7% OF THE POPULATION OF THIS COUNTRY OWNS 84% OF THE WEALTH.

7:84 Theatre Company (Scotland) Ltd presents

# Borderland

## by Andrew Doyle

Commissioned and originally produced by 7:84 Theatre Company (Scotland)

## Cast

Ciarán  **Michael Condron**
Seán  **Richard Orr**
The Clock  **Gareth Morrison**

## Crew

Director  **Lorenzo Mele**
Designer  **Becky Minto**
Production Manager & Lighting Designer  **Dave Shea**
Video Artist  **Fifty-Nine Ltd**
Technical Stage Manager  **Ian Dow**
Company Stage Manager  **Jessica Richards**
Stage Manager  **Vicky Wilson**
Fight Director  **Raymond Short**
Scenic Artist  **Julie Kirsop**
Set Build  **J & B Scenery**
Original Image  **Eamon Melaugh**
Graphic Design  **Neil McGuire**

**Borderland** opened at Paisley Arts Centre on Friday 23 September 2005.

It then toured to Ballachuilish, Aberdeen, Inverness, Glasgow, Musselburgh, Cumbernauld, Birnam, Dunfermline, Stirling, Kilmarnock, Livingston and Dundee.

# Writer's Note

This is an important time for Irish politics. The IRA has finally committed to decommissioning, and has stated that the war is well and truly over. Over a number of years, Gerry Adams has coaxed the IRA into rejecting its most deeply held principles. The IRA's Green Book, a kind of initiation manual, explicitly states that there can be no decommissioning of arms until the ultimate goal of a unified Ireland has been realised. Moreover, the very idea of Sinn Fein taking seats in Stormont flies in the face of the sacrosanct notion of abstentionism. It's nothing short of astounding.

In writing *Borderland*, I was keen to explore this journey from the Armalite to the ballot box, but through the personal story of a fervent republican. It's about the politicisation of death, and what that means to the people involved. So this isn't really a play about the IRA at all, it's about confronting the realities of death, and acknowledging that 'political violence' is an oxymoron.

The play is set after the murder of Robert McCartney, but before the Army Council's announcement. So although the title *Borderland* locates the play geographically, it also intimates this period of transition. The romantic ideal of the IRA volunteer has been sullied by the recent exposure of criminality within the organisation. In turn, the republican movement has been forced to question the legitimacy of death as a political tool. *Borderland* explores these shifting perceptions through the story of two brothers as they struggle to adapt in changing times.

Andrew Doyle
Autumn 2005

# Cast and Crew Biographies

## Michael Condron  *Ciarán*

Michael was born in Toronto and now lives in Belfast. He trained at the University of Ulster, Coleraine. Michael has performed at the Lyric Theatre Belfast in A VERY WEIRD MANOR, CHARLOTTE'S WEB, JOHN BULL'S OTHER ISLAND and CHRISTMAS EVE CAN KILL YOU. His other theatre credits include: THE THREEPENNY OPERA (Bruiser Theatre Company), REVENGE (Tinderbox Theatre Company), COLLEEN BAWN (Big Telly Theatre Company), MOJO MICKYBO (Kabosh Theatre Company), ALMOST HUMAN (Replay Theatre Company) and A FUNNY THING HAPPENED ON THE WAY TO PLANTATION (Edinburgh Fringe Festival). His film, television and radio credits include: JOHNNY WAS, JUST THE JOB (Stirling Productions), PULLING MOVES, I WAS THE CIGARETTE GIRL (BBC NI) and REVENGE (BBC Radio 3).

## Andrew Doyle  *Writer*

Andrew is a playwright, sketch writer, and stand-up comedian. He recently completed his doctoral thesis 'Shakespeare and his contemporaries' at Oxford University, where he was also a part-time lecturer.

**Borderland** is Andrew's first professional commission for the stage. His other plays include: ASCENSION (1998), THE FIRE-BREATHERS (1999), ANOTHER LOVELACE (1999), REDWOMAN (1999), COCKFIGHT (2002), SHAMLET (2003) and THE HIDDEN WINTER (2005).

His short play WAR ON MUCKLE ROE ('a twenty-first century Dad's Army' – *The Herald*) was staged recently by 7:84 at the Traverse Theatre in Edinburgh, as part of a collection of twelve new short plays in response to the global war on terror. Other contributors included David Greig and Naomi Wallace

As a stand-up comedian, Andrew has appeared at The Stand Comedy Club (Edinburgh), Downstairs at the King's Head (London), the Ginglik (London), the Canal Café Theatre (London), and the Gilded Balloon (Edinburgh Fringe Festival).

His new sketch show, CHRISTIE AND DOYLE'S AXIS OF EVIL (co-written with Bridget Christie) enjoyed a successful run at the Underbelly during the 2005 Edinburgh Fringe Festival. He has also written for NEWSREVUE, the political satire show that holds the Guinness World Record for the Longest Running Live Comedy Show.

## Ian Dow *Technical Stage Manager*

Ian graduated from RSAMD in 2000. Since then he has worked with various venues including Dundee Rep, Pitlochry Festival Theatre and the Traverse Theatre, Edinburgh. Ian has worked with 7:84 on BOILING A FROG, PRIVATE AGENDA, GILT, CAN'T PAY? WON'T PAY!, FACTORY GIRLS and CAVE DWELLERS. His other recent work includes: AFTER THE END (Paines Plough and The Bush Theatre at the 2005 Edinburgh Festival), TICKETS PLEASE (Giant Productions) and the touring production of GISELLE (Fabulous Beast Dance Company). Ian was Production Manager on ONE TWO... (Suspect Culture) and UP THE STAIRS AND IN THE ATTIC (Giant Productions).

## Lorenzo Mele *Director*

Since joining 7:84 in 2003, Lorenzo has directed TIPPING POINT, BOILING A FROG, GODEATGOD, PRIVATE AGENDA, THE TRIAL – HOW NEW LABOUR PURGED GEORGE GALLOWAY and two rehearsed readings at the Traverse Theatre of plays by new writers emerging from 7:84's 2003 Writers Summer School. Lorenzo also created GLOBAL RESPONSE which was a rehearsed reading event working with new and established international writers examining the effect of the ongoing war on terror since 9/11. He also directed LAST TUESDAY by Donald Margulies as part of the Amnesty Benefit Night at the Tron Theatre in June 2004. Lorenzo's future plans for the company include the excellent new play FREE FALL by Christopher Deans which was nominated for the Verity Bargate award and will be touring throughout Scotland in Spring 2006.

## Becky Minto *Set Designer*

Becky trained in Interior Design at Liverpool College and in Theatre Design at The Welsh College of Music and Drama. She works throughout Scotland as a Designer and Scenic Artist. Recent productions include: BOILING A FROG (7:84 Theatre Company), BEAUTY AND THE BEAST (The Byre Theatre), MANCUB and LOST ONES (Vanishing Point), SIX BLACK CANDLES (Royal Lyceum Theatre), FIERCE: AN URBAN MYTH (Grid Iron), THE EMPERORS NEW KILT and ARTHUR, THE STORY OF A KING (Wee Stories – Best Children's Show – TMA Awards and Critics Awards for Theatre in Scotland 2004).

Future projects include THE MARSH KING'S DAUGHTER (Byre Theatre) and SPENDING FRANK (Borderline Theatre Company).

### Gareth Morrison  The Clock

Gareth's recent theatre work includes: A MIDSUMMER NIGHT'S DREAM (Brunton Theatre), THE KARAOKE SHOW (Blazin Saddles Productions), PIRATES OF PENZANCE (Citizens Theatre), ANIMAL and HUNCHBACK OF NOTRE DAME (Path Head Arts), TARTUFFE and ENGAGED (Perth Theatre), DON GIOVANNI (Scottish Opera) and GREAT EXPECTATIONS, RESTORATION COMEDY (SYT).

His recent film work include: BROKEN ENGAGEMENT, SOLID AIR, BILL'S FRIEND & 500 YEARS and on television Gareth has appeared in UK EXPO (Fox Network), YOU GOT TO DO THIS (Grampian TV), THE PLAN MAN (SMG) and MONARCH OF THE GLEN (Ecosse Films).

### Richard Orr  Seán

Richard trained at Manchester Polytechnic School of Theatre. He is based in Belfast, and has worked for all the major theatre companies in Northern Ireland. His recent theatre includes: UK tour of MOJO MICKEYBO, PLAYBOY OF THE WESTERN WORLD, SHOPPING AND F***ING, the US tour of PHILADELPHIA, HERE I COME, NEW YEAR'S EVE CAN KILL YOU and JOHN BULL'S OTHER ISLAND. In 2004 he spent five months in Washington DC playing Pavel in FATHERS AND SONS and later in the year he played Andy Warhol in EDIE – A LIVE SHOW ABOUT A DEAD GIRL. Richard's previous work in Scotland includes: Borderline Theatre Company's production of PASSING PLACES and 'TIS PITY SHE'S A WHORE & KING LEAR for Theatre Babel. His TV work includes: EUREKA ST, I FOUGHT THE LAW, GIVE MY HEAD PEACE, TRAIL OF GUILT and THE VIKINGS. His film work includes: CROSS MA HEART, ON DANGEROUS GROUND, MOST FERTILE MAN IN IRELAND, HOOD FELT HATE, MAD ABOUT MAMBO, THE MAGNIFICENT AMBERSONS, BEST and TITANIC TOWN.

### Jessica Richards  *Company Stage Manager*

Jess has worked on TIPPING POINT, REASONS TO BE CHEERFUL, GILT, FACTORY GIRLS and CAVE DWELLERS (7:84 Theatre Company), THREE THOUSAND TROUBLED THREADS, SWEET FANNY ADAMS IN EDEN and WIT (Stellar Quines), THE PRIME OF MISS JEAN BRODIE (Royal Lyceum, Edinburgh), RUNNING GIRL (Boilerhouse) and for the past four years Jess has worked on the pantomime at the Kings Theatre, Glasgow.

**Dave Shea** *Production Manager and Lighting Designer*

Dave's lighting design work includes: TIPPING POINT, BOILING A FROG, PRIVATE AGENDA, SEXSHUNNED, REASONS TO BE CHEERFUL, IT IS DONE, CAN'T PAY? WON'T PAY!, FACTORY GIRLS, CAVE DWELLERS, HOSTAGES TO FEAR, GOLDIE AND THE BEARS and A LITTLE RAIN (7:84 Theatre Company), THE GOLDEN ASS (Suspect Culture), OUR BAD MAGNET (Borderline/Tron Theatre Company), JACK AND THE BEANSTALK, LOVE FREAKS (Tron Theatre Company) and SOMEONE WHO'LL WATCH OVER ME (Company Theatre). He has also designed for Big Like Texas, Ghostown, RSAMD, Complete Productions and Stride Productions. Dave is Production Manager and resident Lighting Designer for 7:84 Theatre Company.

**Vicky Wilson** *Stage Manager*

Vicky studied at Edinburgh's Telford College gaining an HNC in Technical Theatre before attending the RSAMD, graduating in 2003 with a BA in Technical and Production Arts. Vicky has previously worked with 7:84 Theatre Company on BOILING A FROG, PRIVATE AGENDA and REASONS TO BE CHEERFUL. Her recent work includes: AUNTIE JANET SAVES THE PLANET (Scottish Opera For All), 2003 ESTAITES, THE DAWN (Nomad Productions), JEKYL & HYDE (The Theatre Royal), the ACE Project at Paisley University and The Buckie Arts Festival.

**Fifty Nine Ltd** *Video Artists*

Following the huge success of Stellar Quines' production of SWEET FANNY ADAMS IN EDEN and Wee Stories' ARTHUR: THE STORY OF A KING in 2003, Fifty Nine set out to further develop its multimedia services for theatre.

Working within both the financial and technical restraints that usually undermine attempts to use video and film effectively in theatres, the Fifty Nine team has worked on projects where the use of digital technology has become an integral part of the storytelling.

Recent collaborators include Stellar Quines Theatre Company, the Citizens' Theatre, TAG Theatre Company, Grid Iron Theatre Company, Wee Stories, the Scottish Theatre Consortium, the Royal National Theatre and Royal Scottish Academy of Music & Drama. In addition to work in the performing arts, Fifty Nine runs busy units specialising in film production, and graphic design. Read about their range of national and international projects at www.fifty-nine.com.

# 7:84 Theatre Company

Formed in 1973 and based on socialist principles, 7:84 is Scotland's foremost political touring theatre company. The company is committed to producing high quality drama that entertains and politically energises audiences across Scotland. The backbone 7:84 since inception has been to increase access to theatre for those geographically or economically disadvantaged.

> Without living political theatre in Scotland the only voice heard would be the dismal, obedient voice of our media. Without 7:84, or something very like it, communities the length and breadth of Scotland would be excluded from political discourse
>
> *Ian Bell, The Sunday Herald*

7:84 revolutionised the concept of theatre by touring entertaining, topical and political work to places which had never accessed theatre before, most famously through the first production, *The Cheviot, The Stag and the Black, Black Oil*.

Currently the company produces three productions annually, which tour extensively across the length and breadth of Scotland.

Contributing to the professional touring work is the Outreach and Community Action department which delivers ongoing programmes of workshops and mounts two full scale productions per year. With a reputation for excellence, the aim of outreach work is to give a voice to disenfranchised communities by exploring issues both relevant and pertinent.

7:84 are committed to developing political writing. Commissioning work from new and established writers has been a core principle of the company for many years.

More information on the company can be found at www.784theatre.com

Chair **Chris Bartter**
Artistic Director **Lorenzo Mele**
General Manager **Ruth Ogston**
Outreach and Community Action Director **Claire O'Hara**
Production Manager **Dave Shea**
Marketing and Education Manager **Marianne Maxwell**
Outreach and Community Action Officer **Alana Brady**
Administrative Officer **Margaret Bell**

7:84 would like to extend their sincere thanks to Eamon Melaugh, Nell McCafferty, Lalor Roddy, Vincent Higgins, David Ireland, Paisley Arts Centre and Fran Craig.

7:84 Theatre Company are based at
333 Woodlands Road
Glasgow, G3 6NG.
Contact us on 0141 334 6686
or admin@784theatre.com

*Free Mailing List*

You can join our free mailing list by sending your name, address, postcode and telephone number to:
7:84 Theatre Company Scotland
FREEPOST SCO4985
Glasgow, G3 6BR
or by visiting our web site at
www.784theatre.com

7:84 Theatre Company are supported by
The Scottish Arts Council
Glasgow City Council and
Esmée Fairbairn Foundation

# BORDERLAND

First published in 2005 by Oberon Books Ltd
521 Caledonian Road, London N7 9RH
Tel: 020 7607 3637 / Fax: 020 7607 3629
e-mail: oberon.books@btinternet.com
www.oberonbooks.com

A catalogue record for this book is available from the British
Library.

ISBN: 1 84002 605 7

Cover photograph by Eamon Melaugh

Printed in Great Britain by Antony Rowe Ltd, Chippenham.

# CHARACTERS

SEÁN
thirty-eight

CIARÁN
his brother, thirty-one

THE CLOCK
a killer

The play is set in the spring of 2005.

Act One is set in Derry, Northern Ireland.

Act Two is set in Donegal, Republic of Ireland.

# ACT ONE

## Scene One

*Someone's point of view is projected onto a screen upstage, through what appears to be a series of portholes. We see an Irish nationalist mural in the Bogside in Derry, depicting a petrol bomber. Although distorted by the relentless jogging up and down of the projection, the image is reasonably clear. We can hear the sound of heavy breathing, as though someone is exhausted, accompanied by ominous music. The viewer walks past the mural and heads towards a block of flats with a distinctly unsavoury look. It enters and travels upstairs, finally reaching a room. A hand is seen holding out a key and opening the door. The viewer, now clearly some kind of creature in a box, is placed in a cupboard with a view of the room. The creature sees CIARÁN close the cupboard. The projection fades slowly. There is a brief silence before the lights are raised on stage. CIARÁN is sitting on a dilapidated sofa, attempting to learn Braille from a book. He is feeling the pages with his fingers, occasionally closing his eyes and mouthing the words to test himself. A bookcase adorns the wall upstage left, next to a desk strewn with papers and stationery. In the opposing corner of the room is a kitchenette, with basic appliances and some items of food left out to fester. SEÁN storms in, evidently annoyed. He is carrying a Chinese take-away.*

**Ciarán**  You took your time.

**Seán**  I'm here now, amn't I?

*SEÁN removes his jacket and shoes.*

**Ciarán**  *(Feeling the paper again, writing the letters down as he does so.)* G… E… B. *(Pause.)* No, N.

**Seán**  Them weans have got wile cocky.

**Ciarán**  What weans?

**Seán**  Them'ens hanging around the Bogside Inn. Wanted me to buy fags for them.

**Ciarán**  Have you really become that approachable all of a sudden? You should do something about that.

**Seán**  Shut it, you wee bastard.

*SEÁN begins to prepare the food, pouring it on plates and gathering cutlery.*

**Ciarán**  Chinese?

**Seán**  Vaguely.

**Ciarán**  Didn't you get chopsticks?

**Seán**  (*As though addressing a child.*) No. You can't use them, remember? Half your food ends up strewn across your lap.

**Ciarán**  (*Annoyed.*) I can use them.

*SEÁN passes a plate to CIARÁN.*

**Seán**  You can not. You always say you can, but you can't. Just accept it and get on with your life. Use that wee fork there.

**Ciarán**  What's the point of eating Chinese food if you can't use the correct implements?

**Seán**  Give it a rest, for fuck's sake. Did you get the parcel?

**Ciarán**  (*With unconcealed resentment.*) Aye, it's in the press. And there's the usual letter from your man Malachy.

**Seán**  Thanks for doing that, Ciarán.

**Ciarán**  Aye, well.

**Seán**  No I mean it, like. I know how you feel about this stuff.

**Ciarán**  No, you think you know how I feel. You've no idea what it does to me. I was so scared.

**Seán**  There's no reason to be scared, Ciarán. They're on our side.

**Ciarán**  If that's the case they could stand to brush up on their social skills. I was only there ten minutes and I felt like the enemy. You should have seen the way they looked at me. I could feel their eyes on me, groping away. I felt violated.

**Seán**  Well that's you all over, isn't it? Thinking your problems into existence.

**Ciarán**  And the way they stand. They're so, so… predatory. Do you know what I mean? Not at all hospitable.

**Seán**  What did you expect? A red carpet and some vol-au-vents?

**Ciarán**  Well, a cuppa would've been nice.

**Seán**  Jesus.

**Ciarán**  I was parched. It's a steep hill, you know. That reminds me, did you get my mineral water?

*SEÁN takes the bottle of mineral water out of the bag.*

**Seán**  I don't know why you can't drink out of the taps like everyone else.

**Ciarán**  Have you seen the state of those pipes, Seán? It's like Russian roulette every time you brush your teeth.

**Seán**  Well, I like living on the edge.

**Ciarán**  And excuse me, but wasn't it you who claimed that the Brits were putting tranquillizers into our water supply to make us all brain-dead?

**Seán**  All the more reason for you to drink the fucking stuff.

*SEÁN throws the bottle of mineral water to CIARÁN.*

**Ciarán**  Ach Seán, this bottle's got a sports cap. You know I hate these things.

**Seán**  That's all they had. Just drink it, would you?

**Ciarán**  It's like suckling from a sturdy teat. It's a Freudian nightmare.

**Seán**  Why are you doing this to me today? I'm so fucking knackered.

**Ciarán**  It's these Provie mates of yours. They've wound me up, so they have. I'm doing them a favour and they were treating me like shit.

**Seán**  There may be a ceasefire Ciarán, but we're still at war. They've got to be careful. Honest to God, you're that soft.

**Ciarán**  Fine, then don't ask me to do your job. I don't see why you couldn't have done it yourself.

**Seán**  I told you, the Army Council's forbidden it. Everything's suspended for the moment. Smugglings, kneecappings, robberies, the lot of it.

**Ciarán**  If it's supposed to stop then what exactly was I doing today? Because I'm guessing this package isn't a hamper of sponge fancies.

**Seán**  No, it's a delivery.

**Ciarán**  And yet you're telling me the Army Council's holding off for a while.

**Seán**  We have to be cautious. We've taken a beating, what with everything that's been going on this year. Especially in America. Fuck's sake, Adams didn't even get an invite to the White House for Paddy's Day. The whole thing's way out of control.

**Ciarán**  But what is it they're fighting for? All this has done is shown the Provos up for the pack of gangsters they really are.

**Seán**  Don't say that.

**Ciarán**  Why? It's not blasphemous to have an opinion.

**Seán**  Unless it's a blasphemous opinion.

**Ciarán**  You're such a hypocrite. You'll throw your heart and soul into the cause so long as you can keep taking their money.

**Seán**  Just shut up, would you? I told you, you're not to mention that. Ever.

**Ciarán**  (*Looks around.*) There's no one here but us, Seán.

**Seán**  That's not the point. It's dangerous talk.

**Ciarán**  I don't see what's so dangerous about it. Malachy does the deals and takes his own wee cut. And he pays you to be the delivery boy. It all sounds fair enough to me. I shouldn't think the Provos would be all that bothered.

**Seán**  He's a volunteer. Do you understand what that word means?

**Ciarán**  So why are you taking his money?

**Seán**  Because you keep bloody spending it.

**Ciarán**  One day Seán, we'll get ourselves some proper work. And we won't be needing their help anymore. We can be rid of them.

**Seán**  Aye, maybe.

**Ciarán**  It bothers me, you know that? All these deliveries 'n' all. I hate the fact that we're so dependent on Malachy. Ma wouldn't have approved.

**Seán**  Ma's dead, Ciarán.

*A beat.*

**Ciarán**  I need to concentrate on my Braille.

**Seán**  You can't escape it, you know. We're Republicans by birth. It's in our blood.

**Ciarán**  Seán, it's a waste. The lot of it. When my Da left that night with Malachy it was the beginning of the end for us. How can you say that was worthwhile?

**Seán**  The barracks were damaged. And he got himself a kill.

**Ciarán**  Two kills, remember? He didn't come back. An 'own goal', isn't that what yous call it?

**Seán**  A casualty of war, Ciarán. Buried with full honours. Don't you disrespect him like that.

**Ciarán**  I'm doing no such thing.

**Seán**  No? If he could hear the way you're talking he'd fucking disown you.

**Ciarán**  He can't hear me though, can he? That's the point.

**Seán**  You weren't at that funeral. You didn't see all the admiration, the pride. They called him a hero.

**Ciarán**  What kind of hero leaves his two weans in the care of a psychotic mother?

**Seán**  What's that to do with it? He died for Ireland.

**Ciarán**  Like his father. And his father's father. Where does it end, do you see what I'm saying? You can't resent me because you're still alive. Martyrdom is overrated.

**Seán**  (*With contempt.*) You don't understand anything, do you? You're so blinkered.

**Ciarán**  Our grandfather gets a bullet in the neck attacking some RUC outpost in Swatragh. And what for? A shitty wee border campaign that no one takes seriously. Tell me, how does that achieve anything?

**Seán**  On you go, then. Turn your back on your family as well. It's sickening, so it is.

**Ciarán**  (*With scorn.*) Is it?

**Seán**  Catch yourself on. You should be proud. And I should have joined up years ago.

**Ciarán**  Ach, the 'RA wouldn't have someone like yourself.

**Seán**  (*Incensed.*) Shut the fuck up, would you? Of course they'd fucking have me. It's only 'cause of you that I've not been able to join. You realise that, don't you? You drag me down. You're like a fucking dead-weight.

**Ciarán**  If it's really me that's kept you from an early grave then I'm happy enough with that. Believe me.

**Seán**  Who wouldn't die for his country?

**Ciarán**  You wouldn't. I know you wouldn't. You're all bark.

**Seán**  You think you know me so well, don't you?

**Ciarán**  (*With a slight suggestion of a smile.*) You know I do.

*A beat.*

**Seán**  (*Snapping.*) Eat your food.

*CIARÁN pushes the plate away.*

**Ciarán**  I've lost my appetite.

*SEÁN stares at him incredulously.*

**Seán**  You're a wee bugger, you are.

*CIARÁN folds his arms as a gesture of defiance. There is an uncomfortable silence.*

Look, I've been told that this is going to be the last job for a while, right? I'll deliver the package, collect our money from Malachy and make damn certain it lasts. That means cutting back to two meals per day, alright?

*CIARÁN looks at the plate he has pushed away.*

**Ciarán**  I'll die from malnutrition.

**Seán**  Then at least I'll have something else to eat.

**Ciarán**  If you're to be out of work I may as well warn you now that I'm going to be pretty insufferable. I don't take well to poverty.

**Seán**  Then you'll have to change. Maybe get a job yourself for once.

**Ciarán**  But there's no jobs in this town, Seán. Not for the likes of us. That's why everyone with half a brain leaves.

*He wanders over to the mirror and examines his reflection. SEÁN carries on eating.*

When did I disappear? Who the hell is this man I'm looking at? An unemployed Catholic from the Bog, living off the Provos and the DLA. What kind of life is that? (*Pause.*) Christ, I'm getting crows' feet.

**Seán**  Ach, it's just a trick of the light.

**Ciarán**  It's happening already, isn't it?

**Seán**  Get some moisturiser if it bothers you.

**Ciarán**  That's not the point. Decay is contagious. And this place is infected.

**Seán**  What place?

**Ciarán**  Where do you think? Here. The Bogside. It's an infection. Everyone's claiming benefits, nobody calls on the police if there's a problem, I don't know anyone with a TV licence. We're still trying to live outside the system, do you see what I'm saying?

**Seán**  Maybe it's the system that's infected.

**Ciarán**  It's not the system, it's the Bog. Everything's back to front. There's something not quite right when Irish Catholics start marking their territory with Palestinian flags.

**Seán**  They're flying the Israeli flag over in the Fountain.

**Ciarán**  So what? The Prods are just as bad. We're all in the same boat. We're just rowing in different directions.

*He looks back in the mirror.*

**Ciarán**  Oedipus Tyrannus.

**Seán**  What?

**Ciarán**  Greek tragedy. Sophocles. You familiar?

**Seán**  You are such a ponce.

*CIARÁN turns and addresses SEÁN directly.*

**Ciarán**  See the city of Thebes is in a state of decay. Disease, deformity, you name it.

**Seán**  Christ, you and your fucking books.

**Ciarán**  And your man Oedipus is going about his kingly business within the city walls. You know, giving alms and opening shopping centres 'n' all. But what he doesn't know is that the man he killed on the road to Thebes was his own Da. So now this plague has ravaged the city. And everyone's fucked.

**Seán**  You're doing it again.

**Ciarán**  Doing what?

**Seán**  Disappearing up your own arse.

**Ciarán**  Don't be like that. It's an analogy.

**Seán**  A what?

**Ciarán**  We're living in this state of infection because of other people's sins. Derry is suffering from a…from a legacy of perversion. You know I saw a dog in the Brandywell the other day with udders? Udders, for God's sake. They were trailing along the ground. It's an abomination, so it is. Gives me the creeps.

*CIARÁN notices that SEÁN is ignoring him.*

**Ciarán**  I'm sorry, Seán.

**Seán**  What for?

**Ciarán**  For whining. You must be weary of me.

**Seán**  I am, actually.

*CIARÁN withdraws and pours himself a drink. There is a pause.*

**Ciarán**  Sherry?

**Seán**  (*Not lifting his eyes.*) Fuck off.

**Ciarán**  Right.

*SEÁN eats another mouthful. CIARÁN goes back to his Braille.*

**Seán**  These wee noodles taste like shite. What we need here in Derry is a few Chinese people working in the Chinese take-away.

**Ciarán**  Or a few Chinese people at all. A wee bit of ethnic diversity would be nice.

**Seán**  We've got ethnic diversity. Catholics and Protestants.

**Ciarán** (*Feeling the paper again.*) I… D… E. Genocide. (*Pause, then baffled.*) Genocide? My God Seán, look at this.

**Seán** (*Irritated.*) What?

**Ciarán** This Teach Yourself Braille book. This word here is 'genocide'. Morbid, isn't it?

**Seán** I like it.

**Ciarán** What? Genocide?

**Seán** Not the concept. The word. (*Speaking softly with a smile.*) 'Genocide.' Sort of trips off the tongue, doesn't it?

**Ciarán** Couldn't tell you, Seán.

**Seán** What are you learning that stuff for anyway?

**Ciarán** In case I ever go blind.

*SEÁN throws him a look.*

Oh, before I forget.

*CIARÁN casually tosses an envelope over to SEÁN.*

**Seán** What's this?

**Ciarán** You know fine rightly what it is. It came with the box. Time. Location. Et cetera.

**Seán** Oh.

*SEÁN opens the envelope and reads the paper inside. CIARÁN continues to practise his Braille.*

Ciarán.

**Ciarán** Don't even bother.

**Seán** What do you mean?

**Ciarán** I know what you're going to say.

**Seán**  No you don't. You can't possibly know.

**Ciarán**  You're going to ask me to deliver the package for you.

**Seán**  Okay, so you do know.

**Ciarán**  It's out of the question.

**Seán**  Ciarán, be reasonable. I mean, if it's going to be the last for a good while, then…

**Ciarán**  Absolutely not.

**Seán**  (*Pause.*) Ah, come on.

**Ciarán**  No.

**Seán**  Just this once.

**Ciarán**  No.

**Seán**  Never again, I swear it.

**Ciarán**  Just leave me alone, would you? You've already put me at risk, isn't that enough?

**Seán**  How have I put you at risk?

**Ciarán**  That package. It could be a bomb for all I know.

**Seán**  It's not a bomb.

**Ciarán**  Could be.

**Seán**  No Ciarán, it couldn't. Those days are long gone. They'll be selling something on, that's all. Same aul' routine.

*SEÁN stands and lights a cigarette.*

**Ciarán**  Take that outside. You know how I feel about your smoking.

**Seán**  Why don't you go outside?

**Ciarán**  Oh, for God's sake.

**Seán**  It's my house, Ciarán. I pay the rent. Maybe if you earned your keep once in a while.

**Ciarán**  I'm not going to do this thing, Seán. I've done what I said I'd do, and that's it over with. If you need your petty revenge then smoke away, but I'm not going to be bullied by you this time.

**Seán**  You're so selfish, you know that?

**Ciarán**  What?

**Seán**  It's a favour, that's all. Just a wee favour.

**Ciarán**  No, Seán. A favour is taking out the bins when they're full, or picking up some milk from the shop. It's not conducting illegal activities for the benefit of the IRA.

**Seán**  I'm too well known. We all are. But you've never been involved, so you're a safe bet. You can travel anywhere you like and you won't have the peelers breathing down your neck.

**Ciarán**  Why does it have to carry on at all? That Malachy's a maverick, so he is. The Army Council have told him to give it a rest.

**Seán**  Aye, but they don't really mean it.

**Ciarán**  What?

**Seán**  They're just keeping the Sinn-ers happy, that's all. They can't afford for us to stop. When the war starts up again we'll not be caught sitting on our arses.

**Ciarán**  Are you really that delusional? You think they'll tell you one thing and mean the opposite?

**Seán**  It's called politics.

**Ciarán**  I'm not getting involved. I don't see why I should.

**Seán** (*Pause.*) Ach, it'd just be this one last time.

*CIARÁN pretends not to listen.*

Thing is Ciarán, if I go deliver this package now and somebody intercepts me, well… You know what'd happen.

*There is a moment's silence. CIARÁN turns to face SEÁN.*

**Ciarán** Don't you ever worry that Malachy might be, well…exactly what he seems to be?

**Seán** What do you mean?

**Ciarán** We're never told what you're delivering, and we don't know who it's going to. There's got to be an ugly side to all this. Something we don't see. Or if we do see it, it'll be on the news. The TV turns everything into a kind of fiction.

**Seán** It's a noble cause, Ciarán.

**Ciarán** This uncertainty will keep me up tonight. I've enough problems with my insomnia. I see monsters in the shadows.

**Seán** You've an overactive imagination.

**Ciarán** I'm creative like.

**Seán** That's just another word for 'queer'.

**Ciarán** You shouldn't have said anything. I won't sleep tonight.

**Seán** Not if you're this determined, no.

**Ciarán** And I'll be lying there, thinking about what you've done, people you've never met but somehow wronged. And sure I'll work it out. All them snippets of information I've heard will suddenly start to mean something.

**Seán**  I hate it when you start to think.

**Ciarán**  (*Pensive.*) All them cryptic conversations with Malachy that I pretended to understand, all the overheard mutterings, the gossip up the Creggan. We're responsible. We're part of it.

**Seán**  (*Sulking.*) You know, I never ask you for anything.

*SEÁN picks up the newspaper and opens it.*

(*Sarcastic.*) Thanks, Ciarán.

*There is a pause.*

**Ciarán**  Look. If I do this thing will that be it over with?

**Seán**  Absolutely.

**Ciarán**  I mean, that'll be me done. Well and truly.

**Seán**  Well and truly.

**Ciarán**  You promise?

**Seán**  Aye.

*A pause. CIARÁN examines SEÁN's expression. He doesn't quite believe him.*

I mean it like.

**Ciarán**  Aye, I'm sure you do. But you're so capricious.

**Seán**  I'm what?

**Ciarán**  Never mind. (*Pause.*) Give me the letter.

*SEÁN is thrilled.*

**Seán**  Happy days. You're a fucking saviour.

**Ciarán**  You owe me one.

**Seán**  Aye, of course.

**Ciarán**  You'll not ask again?

**Seán**  Never again.

**Ciarán**  Sweet suffering Jesus, the things I do for you.

**Seán**  Ciarán?

**Ciarán**  Aye?

**Seán**  Make us a wee cup of tea.

*CIARÁN shakes his head in disbelief.*

**Ciarán**  You're a cheeky fucker, you know that?

*SEÁN smiles broadly.*

**Seán**  Aye, I know.

*CIARÁN mouths an expletive at SEÁN and walks into the kitchenette to prepare his tea. SEÁN gestures towards CIARÁN's plate.*

Are you going to eat your food or are you just going to let it fester?

**Ciarán**  I told you, I've lost my appetite.

**Seán**  (*Picking up the plate.*) May I?

**Ciarán**  On you go.

*SEÁN opens the newspaper, spreads it out on the coffee table and reads as he eats.*

**Seán**  Oh Christ, he's done it again.

**Ciarán**  What's that?

**Seán**  Another killing in Derry. Brendan Flannery from Ballymagroarty.

**Ciarán**  UDA?

**Seán**  No, not paramilitary. It's The Clock.

**Ciarán**  (*Pause.*) The what?

**Seán**  The Clock.

*No reaction from CIARÁN.*

(*Louder.*) The Clock!

**Ciarán**  Aye, I heard you the first time! I know what you said, I don't know what you meant just. Someone was killed by a clock?

**Seán**  Not a clock, you ejit, The Clock.

**Ciarán**  Right. (*Pause.*) You do realise you're making no sense whatsoever.

**Seán**  Are you for real?

**Ciarán**  I mean, don't get me wrong. It's quite a skill, such persistent incoherence. I don't know how you sustain it.

**Seán**  Have you not heard of The Clock?

**Ciarán**  No I have not. Do enlighten me.

**Seán**  Well where the fuck have you been? He's the serial killer.

**Ciarán**  I didn't think we got serial killers in the north. We've enough lunatics already.

**Seán**  You must have heard of him.

**Ciarán**  I don't read the papers. They upset me.

**Seán**  He's a right vicious bastard. The press are loving it, so they are. See this fella's got a system.

**Ciarán**  What do you mean?

**Seán**  Once he's chosen his victim, he waits until they're alone one evening, then breaks in and cripples them.

**Ciarán**  A kneecapping?

**Seán**  Not a gun. Something else.

**Ciarán**  What?

**Seán**  I don't know. It doesn't matter. (*Enjoying telling the story.*) Anyway, he doesn't kill his victims straight away, see? He cripples them, and walks away for a while, before coming back to finish the job. He leaves a wee clock in the room set on an hour timer, so his victims can literally watch the countdown to their deaths. And when the clock strikes…The Clock strikes.

**Ciarán**  It all sounds rather melodramatic to me.

**Seán**  Tell that to O'Connell.

**Ciarán**  Who?

**Seán**  For God's sake, Ciarán. You've the memory of a salmon. Colm O'Connell. Lived on our street. Scrawny. Blonde. Frantic.

**Ciarán**  I remember a scrawny man, a blonde man and a frantic man on our street. But I can't reconcile the three into one person.

**Seán**  I saved the obituary for you.

**Ciarán**  You never gave it to me.

**Seán**  Did I not? Hang on.

*SEÁN walks to the sideboard and rummages amongst the papers. He finds the cutting he is looking for and hands it to CIARÁN.*

Third column.

**Ciarán**  I don't remember him.

**Seán**  You must do. Think carefully. (*Pause.*) Colm O'Connell. Stuttered a bit. You must remember him.

**Ciarán**  Honestly Seán, I don't know who you mean.

**Seán**  (*Getting increasingly impatient.*) Colm O'Connell! Had a nervous breakdown after he was interned. They said it was the white noise that done it.

**Ciarán**  A volunteer, was he?

**Seán**  Aye. Joined up after Bloody Sunday.

**Ciarán**  Was he hunched?

**Seán**  That's the one.

**Ciarán**  Oh, you mean Humpy O'Connell? Why didn't you say?

*There is a pause. SEÁN is not impressed by this lack of respect.*

**Seán**  You know he was shot twice by the LVF. We thought he was invincible.

*SEÁN reverts to reading his newspaper.*

There's no justice. He lives through two attacks from loyalist death squads, and gets clobbered by a fucking head-case with no interest in Irish politics at all.

**Ciarán**  Here's your tea.

**Seán**  Thanks.

*He takes a sip.*

That's dead on.

*CIARÁN looks over SEÁN's shoulder at the newspaper.*

**Ciarán**  So this Clock character? He did Humpy O'Connell?

**Seán**  Aye.

**Ciarán**  When did this happen?

**Seán**  Dunno. Couple of months ago or something. He was the eighth victim. I can't believe you haven't heard about all this.

**Ciarán**  Well I haven't. Just let it pass.

**Seán**  (*Indicating his newspaper.*) You'll be reading this after me. You need to be educated.

**Ciarán**  I'm learning Braille, amn't I?

**Seán**  You want to wise up, Ciarán. You're a time-waster, so you are.

*CIARÁN takes the newspaper from SEÁN.*

**Ciarán**  (*Reading.*) 'The Clock Strikes Again.' Have they been using that pun a lot, then?

**Seán**  Ad nauseam.

**Ciarán**  There's no pictures of him.

**Seán**  He's a murderer. He doesn't stick around for the press coverage.

**Ciarán**  'So far the killer has evaded the authorities, despite the PSNI's recent pledge to make his arrest their utmost priority. Flannery is the thirteenth victim in the series of killings, each one progressively more brutal than the last. James Shilling, the sole survivor of an attack described his assailant as five foot ten, of large build, wearing a black balaclava.' Sounds paramilitary to me.

**Seán**  Well it isn't.

**Ciarán**  Someone escaped him, then?

**Seán**  That's right. Over in County Down. Managed to crawl down the stairwell of his block of flats, even with his legs mashed up. Quite an achievement. Sold his story for a wee fortune.

**Ciarán**  And what about your man O'Connell? Was he in Malachy's company?

**Seán**  Aye. They were friends. It's one big happy family.

**Ciarán**  They'll be looking for him.

**Seán**  Of course they'll be looking for him. Six of his victims have been Catholics. Two of them active Republicans. They'll find him and they'll kill him. Peace process or no.

**Ciarán**  Six Catholics? Who were the others?

**Seán**  Prods. Seven of 'em.

**Ciarán**  Well it doesn't sound sectarian to me.

**Seán**  That hardly matters. There's two dead Provos here. Malachy'll see to him.

**Ciarán**  I suppose this fella should have realised who he was dealing with.

**Seán**  I very much doubt he cares. He's a lunatic. Gets a kick out of death.

**Ciarán**  So does Malachy.

**Seán**  But Malachy's not a lunatic.

**Ciarán**  I wouldn't be so sure about that.

*CIARÁN drops the newspaper into SEÁN's lap.*

Why have we willingly consigned ourselves to a world of lunacy? We don't belong and we never did. Everything feels wrong at the moment. Don't you sense it?

**Seán**  What are you going on about now?

**Ciarán**  You know I was walking down Shipquay Street one morning last week, looking for cough drops, when this aul' woman in an electric wheelchair stopped me and asked the time. And I didn't like the look of her, so I pretended not to have a watch. She had this growth on her neck. Like a second head, only smaller and featureless. So I say to her, this deformed crippled woman, I say, 'I dunno, sorry.'

**Seán**  How long is this going to take?

**Ciarán**  (*Ignoring him.*) She doesn't budge but. She just sits there, looking up at me with them big brown eyes. Piercing into me like fucking needles, so that it actually hurts me to look at her. But then it gets so uncomfortable that I try to walk away, only she rolls on after me. I can hear the purring of her wee engine, and I feel obliged to stop. When she gets close enough, she actually reaches up and grabs my arm, pulling back the sleeve to get a look at my watch. It's as though she knew I was lying all along. And I'm suddenly terrified of what her reaction's going to be. Imagine that. Me, scared of some misshapen aul' woman. It's not as though she could've done me any damage.

**Seán**  Oh, I don't know. She could have run over your feet.

**Ciarán**  (*Ignoring him.*) I guess I just didn't want to hurt her feelings. Maybe it's as simple as that. I felt ashamed that I hadn't told her the time when she asked. It made me feel even worse when, having seen that it was ten o'clock, she just rolled away without a word, or even a disapproving glance over her shoulder.

**Seán**  Maybe her second head would have got in the way.

**Ciarán**  It wasn't actually a second head, it was a growth.

**Seán**  Whatever.

**Ciarán**  Perhaps she cursed me. I've had a bad feeling from the moment I got the package.

**Seán**  (*Disdainful.*) You really think you're cursed?

**Ciarán**  Maybe. I shouldn't be trying to hide time from anyone. No one's exempt from that particular burden.

**Seán**  Wind your neck in, Ciarán. I'm bored with this shite.

**Ciarán**  I didn't want to talk to her because she was ugly. What does that say about me?

**Seán**  That you're too honest with yourself. Get the package.

**Ciarán**  And now this nauseous feeling again. It's been happening all the time these days. What does it mean?

**Seán**  Well maybe you are ill, after all.

**Ciarán**  I know, I shouldn't be but. I've been taking multi-vitamins.

**Seán**  That doesn't guarantee a long life.

**Ciarán**  Can't hurt. (*Pause.*) Do you think I'm dying?

**Seán**  Ciarán, what are you drivelling about?

**Ciarán**  Well since my Ma died I've never been in good health. Literally never. Colds, fevers, allergies, there's always something.

**Seán**  Aye, something for you to complain about.

**Ciarán**  (*Distant.*) And Death's always there, lurking at the borders, waiting. (*Pause, a panicky realisation.*) He could be taking me right now, couldn't he? My cells could be ravaged by cancer. I could be rotting away within and I'd never know. Not until it's too late. (*Pause.*) That's a scary concept.

*CIARÁN realises that SEÁN is paying no attention.*

Couldn't you put that down for a moment? Look at me.

**Seán**  (*Not looking.*) Mmm?

*CIARÁN grabs the paper, storms over to the bin and thrusts it in.*

**Ciarán**  Look at me, Seán. Interaction, you see? It takes two at the very least.

**Seán**  Far be it for me to raise the obvious, but you seemed quite happy in your wee monologue. You tend to blather, Ciarán. It's not entertaining, I promise you. Now give me my fucking paper back before I break your arms.

*He does so.*

What time is it?

**Ciarán**  Seven. You'd better get ready.

**Seán**  Don't you do that. You said you'd do this for me, you can't go back on it now.

**Ciarán**  Seán, I'm having second thoughts. More to the point, I really do feel sick. I mean it like.

**Seán**  This is absurd. You made a promise.

**Ciarán**  I didn't.

**Seán**  You fucking did.

**Ciarán**  Now, Seán…

**Seán**  I'm not discussing it with you, Ciarán. You said you'd do it, so you're doing it. And remember, this is going to be the last one for a good long while, so you'd better be on the ball. Like a bloody performing dog.

**Ciarán**  I'd sooner not perform at all. Where's your empathy? I'm unwell.

**Seán**  You're dead on. Your cheeks are so rosy you look like a fucking cartoon character.

**Ciarán**  I feel poised to vomit.

**Seán**  Do so, clean up, make a move.

**Ciarán**  But I'm cursed, so I am. This package. There's something wrong with it. I can feel it.

**Seán**  You're not cursed, Ciarán.

**Ciarán**  Will I make you another cup of tea?

**Seán**  Go fetch the box.

**Ciarán**  I'm really not up for this right now.

**Seán**  (*Slower, threatening.*) Go fetch the box.

*CIARÁN walks to the cupboard and removes the box. The projection begins again, and we see the creature's view of the room. CIARÁN places the box on the table. As he does so, the box shudders visibly. CIARÁN jumps in fright.*

**Ciarán**  Shit! I knew it, it's a fucking bomb!

**Seán**  Don't be daft.

**Ciarán**  It moved. It moved.

**Seán**  Bombs generally explode, they don't just move about the place.

**Ciarán**  Right enough. So what is it?

**Seán**  Look at the wee holes. Doesn't that give you some sort of hint?

**Ciarán**  What do you mean?

**Seán**  Well they're air holes, aren't they? (*Pause.*) For breathing.

**Ciarán**  Do you mean to tell me that there's a wee animal in there?

**Seán**  Well whatever it is, it moves. (*Pause.*) That's strange.

**Ciarán**  I know.

**Seán** There's doing over banks, and there's stealing shipments of fags and booze. I've never heard of the IRA making their money from transporting livestock.

**Ciarán** What about all that sheep-smuggling over the border?

**Seán** (*Thinks about it.*) Aye well, apart from that.

*CIARÁN stares at the box.*

**Ciarán** So very peculiar. (*Pause.*) Shall we have a look?

**Seán** (*Pause.*) No. Just deliver it.

**Ciarán** Aren't you curious?

**Seán** (*Pause.*) I'm not supposed to open the packages I deliver. That's not my job.

**Ciarán** It's not very efficiently sealed but. No one would ever know.

**Seán** Have we ever opened a package before?

**Ciarán** Never.

**Seán** So this is no different. Let's be professional about this.

**Ciarán** Why should we? If I'm to be doing a favour for these fellas they can at least indulge me in this.

**Seán** You say that to Malachy and see how far it gets you.

**Ciarán** Ah, come on. It's not as though anything can go wrong.

**Seán** For a start we don't know what this thing is. It could be a nimble wee bastard. The second you lift that flap it could scurry past you and leave you with a whole bunch of IRA lads on your tail.

**Ciarán** Even if it gets past us, it couldn't leave the flat. All the doors are closed, and the windows don't even open properly. Weren't you supposed to speak to the landlady about that?

**Seán**  Don't change the subject.

**Ciarán**  Well it's a serious fire hazard, and you know I can't talk to women with facial hair.

**Seán**  (*Losing patience.*) Look, I'm not having you open this.

**Ciarán**  (*Childish.*) But Seán, I won't be able to sleep tonight if I don't know what this creature is. I'm going to have to do it. I'm sorry.

**Seán**  Fine. I'm not getting involved.

*SEÁN walks over to the other side of the room.*

**Ciarán**  I'm going in.

**Seán**  Wait.

**Ciarán**  What?

**Seán**  Just think about this for a moment.

**Ciarán**  I thought you didn't want to be involved.

**Seán**  We shouldn't do this. It's prohibited. It goes against everything I stand for.

**Ciarán**  Catch yourself on. You don't stand for anything. You pretend you're a fervent Republican but you don't even know what abstentionism is.

**Seán**  I do so.

**Ciarán**  What is it, then?

**Seán**  (*Pause.*) Why are you always trying to change the subject?

**Ciarán**  All I'm doing is satisfying my curiosity. It's harmless.

**Seán**  But you don't know if the creature is.

**Ciarán**  Look at the size of the box. It's hardly going to be a Bengal tiger, is it?

**Seán**  Okay, I'll hold it but. Knowing you you'd drop the box and break the damn thing's neck. I'll not have you delivering a corpse in my name.

*SEÁN holds the box.*

**Ciarán**  Fine. Ready?

**Seán**  I suppose.

*CIARÁN opens the box. They peer inside. There is a pause. Both men assume utterly blank expressions.*

Ciarán?

**Ciarán**  Seán?

**Seán**  What the fuck is that?

**Ciarán**  Er…I couldn't honestly tell you.

**Seán**  See, this is exactly the reason I didn't want to be involved. I don't want to see things like that.

**Ciarán**  I mean, for God's sake, it's…it's… What are them things on its, on its…whatever it is?

**Seán**  I don't know what the things are, or what the thing is that the things are attached to. Whatever it is, it's wile looking. Close the box, little brother. Get rid of it.

**Ciarán**  It's very docile. Hey, I think it's smiling at me.

**Seán**  Don't talk shite.

**Ciarán**  Look, look.

*SEÁN reluctantly walks to his side.*

That's a smile, right?

**Seán**  Could be. Could be anything. We can't even be sure that's a mouth.

**Ciarán**  It's kind of cute.

**Seán**  What are you talking about? It's weird.

**Ciarán**  She's weird, sure. But there's something about her. Can we give her a name?

**Seán**  Since when did 'it' become 'she'?

**Ciarán**  I'm pretty sure she's female.

**Seán**  We're not naming it. No way. I'm drawing the line.

**Ciarán**  But she looks like a…

**Seán**  No! None of that.

**Ciarán**  Siobhan.

**Seán**  Siobhan? Siobhan? Are you off your fucking nut? (*Pause.*) Let me see.

*SEÁN examines the animal.*

**Ciarán**  Ursula, then.

**Seán**  No, you're right. She is a Siobhan.

**Ciarán**  (*Beaming.*) Excellent.

**Seán**  You see what you've made me do? You've gulled me into a christening.

**Ciarán**  She is beautiful, isn't she? In a really really unorthodox kind of way.

**Seán**  What difference does it make? Close the box.

**Ciarán**  Why? Ach, look, she's licking my finger.

**Seán**  Don't let her do that!

**Ciarán**  She's unlikely to have a poisonous tongue, Seán.

**Seán**  We've no idea what she is.

**Ciarán**  I think it's safe to assume she doesn't have a lethal lick.

**Seán**  Where's that animal book? You know the one with the ripped dust-jacket.

**Ciarán**  No, I got rid of that.

**Seán**  The book or the dust-jacket?

**Ciarán**  The dust-jacket. It was ripped.

**Seán**  I know. I know it was ripped. I don't care about the fucking dust-jacket, I want to know where the book is.

**Ciarán**  Look for the navy blue spine.

**Seán**  Right.

*SEÁN begins to finger the bindings.*

**Ciarán**  Oh no, wait. The dust-jacket was navy blue.

**Seán**  (*Getting exasperated.*) What colour was the book?

**Ciarán**  Green. No, black. Green. Actually, I can't remember.

**Seán**  You really are a useless cunt, aren't you?

**Ciarán**  Well, Siobhan likes me. (*To the animal, in a childish voice.*) Don't you Siobhan? Yes you do, yes you do.

**Seán**  Here it is.

*He flicks through the book slowly, comparing the pictures to the animal in the box.*

**Ciarán**  Stop, what was that one?

**Seán**  A mountain goat.

**Ciarán**  Back a page.

**Seán**  (*Turning the page back.*) That's a gazelle.

**Ciarán**  Oh. It's just the nose looked kind of… Well, you were flicking very fast.

**Seán**  Don't interrupt me. (*Finding a page.*) Here. I knew she looked familiar. (*Holding the book out to CIARÁN.*) There's a slight resemblance, don't you think?

**Ciarán**  A bit, maybe. What is that?

**Seán**  A basilisk.

**Ciarán**  What's one of them?

**Seán**  That's the problem. They're mythical. Never really existed.

*CIARÁN takes the book.*

**Ciarán**  It says here that traditionally it was believed that the basilisk could only be killed by weasels. Interesting bit of trivia.

*SEÁN glares threateningly at CIARÁN.*

Well, might come in handy. For the quiz night at Sean Dolan's.

*SEÁN snatches the book from CIARÁN and slams it shut.*

**Seán**  You've totally screwed things up this time, Pandora.

**Ciarán**  What do you mean?

**Seán**  There was a very good reason why I didn't want you to open this box. You know how sappy you get around animals.

**Ciarán**  Is this really how the Provos are making their money these days? Stealing rare animals and selling them on?

**Seán**  I suppose.

**Ciarán**  That's wile odd.

**Seán** Truly.

**Ciarán** Who would want to buy her?

**Seán** Some rich weirdo probably. I wouldn't be surprised if she's to be skinned.

**Ciarán** Well she's got very soft skin.

**Seán** Exactly.

**Ciarán** Oh God, I won't be able to sleep tonight.

**Seán** You're always saying that, but you always do sleep. Just close the box and get going.

**Ciarán** I think she's hungry.

**Seán** No, Ciarán. She's not.

**Ciarán** How do you know?

**Seán** Close the box.

**Ciarán** I will not.

**Seán** We're not feeding her, Ciarán.

**Ciarán** Pass me that plate.

**Seán** I didn't buy you a Chinese meal so you could use it as pet food.

**Ciarán** Ach, give over. Chuck us a couple of bean sprouts.

**Seán** We shouldn't interfere with the goods.

**Ciarán** The goods? Siobhan's no one's goods. She's a free spirit.

**Seán** Hardly.

**Ciarán** Well she should be.

**Seán** What?

**Ciarán**  I mean, it's not natural, is it? Poor Siobhan, cooped up in this box. It's not right. We should do something about it.

**Seán**  What are you suggesting?

**Ciarán**  You know what I'm suggesting.

**Seán**  Aye I do, and I don't like it.

*SEÁN storms over to the box, closes it, and thrusts it into CIARÁN's arms.*

**Ciarán**  Careful, you'll hurt her. What's the matter with you?

**Seán**  I want it out of here.

**Ciarán**  She's not going anywhere.

**Seán**  Are you seriously suggesting that we should set this animal free? That's fucking suicide.

**Ciarán**  Why not but? Sure this could be our redemption.

**Seán**  (*Genuinely flabbergasted.*) Fuck me. You're a nutcase.

**Ciarán**  What are you worried about? Your man Malachy? Come on, let's do it. Fuck Malachy. Fuck all them bastards. We could let her go down by the grotto. There's plenty of stray dogs round the Brandywell. She might find herself a wee friend.

**Seán**  I cannot believe I am hearing this.

**Ciarán**  She deserves her liberty.

**Seán**  And what do we tell Malachy?

**Ciarán**  We tell him she escaped. That she gnawed through the box and scampered off.

**Seán**  No, Ciarán. No fucking way. It's out of the question.

**Ciarán**  We have a responsibility to Siobhan.

**Seán**  Siobhan won't put a bullet in the back of our heads. Malachy will.

**Ciarán**  I can look after myself.

**Seán**  What are you talking about? I know you, remember?

**Ciarán**  Okay. But between us, we can pull it off.

**Seán**  Go deliver the box. Right now.

**Ciarán**  (*Backing off.*) No.

**Seán**  I hope I didn't hear you right.

**Ciarán**  You heard me right. Siobhan's not going anywhere near them bastards.

**Seán**  (*Approaching CIARÁN.*) Get your arse out of that door now and finish what you started.

**Ciarán**  (*Clearly intimidated.*) But, Seán.

**Seán**  Not another word, okay?

**Ciarán**  But…

*SEÁN pushes him against the wall.*

**Seán**  Not another…word. (*Pause.*) Understand?

*CIARÁN nods.*

I don't like this any more than you do. But it's either her or us.

*CIARÁN places the box carefully on the table.*

**Ciarán**  (*Pause.*) I think I'll take a nap.

*He moves towards the exit.*

**Seán**  No you fucking won't. The rendezvous's over at Sheriff's Mountain.

*CIARÁN turns, reluctantly.*

You haven't got time for a nap. You promised me, Ciarán.

**Ciarán** (*Pause, then resigned.*) Alright.

*CIARÁN picks up the box and starts to exit. SEÁN turns and looks at him.*

**Seán** You going to wear them trainers, are you?

**Ciarán** Why not?

**Seán** It's teemin' out there.

**Ciarán** I'll wear my boots.

*CIARÁN finds his boots and puts them on.*

I'll be away then.

**Seán** Thank Christ. I could do with some peace.

*CIARÁN picks up the box.*

**Ciarán** You want to say goodbye to Siobhan?

**Seán** No.

*SEÁN picks up the letter.*

Sheriff's Mountain. Meeting with a Mr David Grimes.

*He hands CIARÁN the letter.*

**Ciarán** David Grimes. Right.

**Seán** Don't screw this up.

*CIARÁN motions to exit.*

**Ciarán** I won't. You just relax. Finish your Chinese.

**Seán** It's cold now.

**Ciarán** You like it cold.

*CIARÁN exits.*

**Seán**  Aye. I suppose I do.

*SEÁN slumps onto the sofa. Blackout.*

# Scene Two

*The creature's point of view is projected onto the screen. We see the one of the Bogside murals; the civil rights march on Bloody Sunday. The creature begins to scuttle through the streets of the Bogside. Suddenly we see CIARÁN, beaten up, his clothes bloodstained, running as fast as he can. The creature follows him. CIARÁN frequently looks back, anxious. He approaches the outside of his flat, and the creature watches him enter. The lights are raised. CIARÁN enters, gasping for breath.*

**Ciarán**  Seán? Where… (*Coughs.*) Seán. Seán!

*SEÁN enters.*

**Seán**  Oh Christ, what now?

**Ciarán**  (*Agonised.*) Help me.

**Seán**  (*Almost irritated.*) Sit down. I'll get some antiseptic.

*He does so.*

Now what the fuck is this about?

**Ciarán**  I don't understand it. I was on my way back and… Oh Seán, it hurts.

**Seán**  Aye, I'm sure it does. Hold still.

*He starts to apply the antiseptic.*

Where did this happen?

**Ciarán**  (*Still disorientated.*) I don't know. Westland Avenue.

**Seán**  Behind the playground?

**Ciarán**  (*Nods, clutching his head.*) Behind the playground. There were f…four of them.

**Seán**  What do you expect? You shouldn't have gone that way. There are other, safer, routes back from Sheriff's Mountain, you know.

**Ciarán**  It's a playground but!

**Seán**  What does that matter? Remember Chris Phelan? Got stabbed in the head there. Managed to crawl to Nazareth House in time to save his life, but now his face looks like a badly peeled potato.

**Ciarán**  Oh Seán. (*Clutches him.*) It hurts, it really hurts.

**Seán**  Get off me, you girl you. (*Holds CIARÁN's chin up.*) You're fine. A few cuts and bruises just. You'll live. More's the pity.

*SEÁN applies some plasters.*

**Ciarán**  Should we not call a doctor?

**Seán**  What for?

**Ciarán**  They hit me… On the head. (*In sudden shock.*) I could die!

**Seán**  You're not going to die, Ciarán.

**Ciarán**  Can I have a mirror?

**Seán**  I don't think you're quite ready for a mirror yet.

**Ciarán**  (*Panicky.*) Why? Is it bad? Is it really bad?

**Seán**  No. Of course not. I just want to get you cleaned up a bit first.

*CIARÁN curses, stands, and finds a mirror. SEÁN seems exasperated.*

Ciarán, please don't.

*CIARÁN looks in the mirror. He is immediately horrified.*

**Ciarán**  Oh my face. My face. (*Pause.*) It's gone.

**Seán**  It'll grow back.

**Ciarán**  They took my face!

**Seán**  (*Standing.*) Now calm down, for God's sake. You don't even need stitches. Honestly, you're such a drama queen.

**Ciarán**  (*Hurt.*) I'm not.

**Seán**  You are so. Why does it always have to be such a performance with you? You make a song and dance about everything. You should be in a musical.

**Ciarán**  Can I have a sherry?

**Seán**  In a moment. I want to get all the grit out first. Sit down.

*CIARÁN does so. SEÁN begins to dab at his face with cotton wool.*

It's common sense to steer clear of that playground. Everyone knows that. This is your own fault, really.

**Ciarán**  I don't. I had no… Ow! Go easy.

**Seán**  Sorry.

**Ciarán**  I didn't know it was so rough.

**Seán**  Everyone avoids it. Even the lads from Restorative Justice. They've given up trying. Did they take anything from you?

**Ciarán**  No. They just asked me the time then punched me.

**Seán**  It's that digital watch you wear. It's offensive. Can you not hold still? I don't want to make it any worse than it already is.

**Ciarán**  You're enjoying this, aren't you?

**Seán**  Ach, you've got to see the funny side.

**Ciarán**  Well I don't share your sense of humour. This is your fault, you do realise that don't you? See this is exactly why I shouldn't be getting involved.

**Seán**  Calm down, would you? It's not all that bad.

**Ciarán**  I could be damaged for life. They hit me in the head.

**Seán**  So you said.

**Ciarán**  I could have brain damage.

**Seán**  We probably wouldn't notice.

*CIARÁN looks in the mirror again.*

**Ciarán**  My eyes look weird. (*Pause.*) My pupils are like pinpricks. Look, Seán, look. My pupils are practically non-existent. I'm all iris.

**Seán**  Your eyes are fine. Sure the pupils are dilated if anything.

**Ciarán**  (*Alarmed.*) Well what does that mean?

**Seán**  It may mean that this room is on the dim side.

**Ciarán**  Well turn some more lights on!

**Seán**  Ciarán, you're out of control. I will be forced to sedate you.

**Ciarán**  With what?

**Seán**  A mallet. (*Applies the final plaster.*) There. You're done.

*SEÁN stands. CIARÁN seems excessively nervous.*

**Ciarán**  I'll be honest, Seán. I don't think I can stay here anymore.

**Seán**  What do you mean?

**Ciarán**  This flat. This area. I mean it's infected with violence. It seeps and trickles through everything and everyone here. You can practically slip on it.

**Seán**  Try not to be so clumsy, then. All you need to do is avoid a few known trouble spots. Not at all street-wise, are you?

**Ciarán**  I don't see why I should have to be. This isn't what life's about.

**Seán**  What is it about then? What's with this delusion that life is supposed to be easy? Or fun? It's not. It's a series of experiences, mostly awful.

*CIARÁN begins to pace, throwing repeated nervous glances at the door.*

**Ciarán**  Let's get out of here. I hate the Bogside. I hate the Brandywell. I hate the murals and the people and that fucking ugly grotto.

**Seán**  Stop it, Ciarán. You're in pain, that's all. Sure you won't feel like this tomorrow.

**Ciarán**  That's not true. We need to move.

**Seán**  We're not going anywhere.

**Ciarán**  We need to move today.

**Seán**  Why?

**Ciarán**  I'm telling you, this place is infected. It's a plague, and it's spreading.

**Seán**  Fuck up, Ciarán. We're staying here.

**Ciarán**  But them bastards at the playground…

**Seán**  (*Getting impatient.*) What about them?

**Ciarán**  They… I think they followed me.

**Seán**  (*Sarcastic.*) Oh no. We're done for.

**Ciarán**  I'm serious, Seán.

**Seán**  You forget, brother. I'm not the sap that you are. I can look after myself.

**Ciarán**  Look, I'm pleading with you. I can't stay here anymore. I need to move. And I need to move this instant. It's not safe. And I'm wounded.

**Seán**  Aye. And this shite you're spouting is just another symptom. Like the pain. Only more irritating.

**Ciarán**  It was Grimes.

*There is a long pause.*

**Seán**  What did you say?

**Ciarán**  Grimes. Grimes did this to me.

*There is a long pause. SEÁN stares at CIARÁN, threateningly. He takes a step towards him, and CIARÁN backs off.*

Now don't overreact.

**Seán**  What happened?

**Ciarán**  The truth?

**Seán**  Of course the truth.

**Ciarán**  You won't be angry?

**Seán**  Well that depends, doesn't it?

**Ciarán**  I took Siobhan there. Just like you told me to. And they were there. Four of 'em. Looking wile angry. Bastards they were. I could tell straight away. One of them had a tattoo. Some kind of snake.

**Seán**  Why didn't you tell me this before?

**Ciarán**  I'm sorry. I'm just scared is all.

**Seán**  Oh Ciarán, what have you done?

**Ciarán**  (*Unconvincing.*) Nothing. There's nothing to tell.

**Seán**  Ciarán, I'm not joking.

**Ciarán**  What makes you think I am?

*SEÁN grabs CIARÁN by the collar, and pulls him onto the coffee table, pushing down on his neck.*

Stop that! You're hurting me.

**Seán**  I swear to God if you've done anything to piss them off I'll scalp you with a fucking cheese grater.

**Ciarán**  It was his fault.

**Seán**  What was his fault?

**Ciarán**  He said they'd kill her.

**Seán**  Kill who?

**Ciarán**  Siobhan!

*SEÁN releases CIARÁN's neck and takes a pace back, horrified.*

**Seán**  Lord fucking Christ, you are one useless wee fucking bastard who doesn't have the fucking brains you were fucking born with.

**Ciarán**  Eloquent.

*SEÁN grabs CIARÁN by the collar and pushes him against the wall.*

**Seán**  (*Furious.*) What have you done?

**Ciarán**  You were right, Seán. You were joking, but you were right. They're going to kill her. She's going to be a pelt.

**Seán**  A pelt?

**Ciarán**  It's a skin. For decoration and that.

**Seán**  I know what a pelt is. Get to the point.

**Ciarán**  You've got to understand but. Them lads were talking about skinning her alive. It was so horribly sadistic and I just couldn't bear to think of her in such agony.

**Seán**  (*In realisation.*) Oh my God.

**Ciarán**  I had no alternative.

**Seán**  You let her go.

**Ciarán**  (*Nodding.*) I let her go.

*SEÁN slumps down into the sofa.*

**Seán**  I can't be hearing this. You've ruined everything. Everything. Any chance I ever had.

**Ciarán**  Any chance of what?

*SEÁN raises his head slowly, a look of genuine fury on his face.*

**Seán**  You stupid bastard.

**Ciarán**  Seán, I had to. You should have heard what they were saying 'n' all. It was so vicious, so ugly. It wasn't even as though it was a conscious action on my part. My hand just seemed to instinctively reach over to the box and…lift the flap.

**Seán**  I can't believe you. The one thing I ask you to do, the one thing… Well that's it. You've done it. We're dead.

**Ciarán**  Not so. We can leave. We can leave right now.

**Seán**  (*Erupting.*) You really are thick, aren't you? Where the fuck do you think we can go now? What do think we can do? Malachy will have already sent someone here to take care of us.

**Ciarán**  Then we'd better get going, eh?

*SEÁN advances towards CIARÁN, menacingly.*

Look, I accept total responsibility, but you said yourself, they'll be on their way already. You haven't got time to lay into me now.

**Seán**  What were you intending to do? Were you just never going to tell me?

**Ciarán**  I... I wasn't thinking properly. I just knew that you'd be pissed off.

**Seán**  Don't understate the case, Ciarán. I'm fucking furious.

**Ciarán**  I couldn't bring myself to tell you straight away, I just couldn't.

**Seán**  For God's sake, what are you more afraid of? Me or the fucking Irish Republican Army?

**Ciarán**  Well, when you put it like that.

**Seán**  You are such a prick. Get your stuff together.

**Ciarán**  What stuff?

**Seán**  Whatever you can grab in ten seconds. We're leaving.

*SEÁN stuffs a few items into a rucksack and throws a bag at CIARÁN.*

Hurry.

**Ciarán**  I'm... I'm not sure what to take.

**Seán**  Then don't take anything. (*Pushing CIARÁN.*) Let's go.

**Ciarán**  Watch the shoulder! I think it's bruised.

**Seán**  Just move.

*CIARÁN grabs a couple of books as they exit. After a moment, SEÁN runs back in. He kneels on the floor and pulls back the rug. He starts to lift the floorboard but hears CIARÁN approaching. Quickly, he replaces the rug and stands. CIARÁN enters.*

**Ciarán**  Seán, we've got to go. You forgotten something?

*SEÁN glances at the floor.*

**Seán**  No. (*Pause.*) No, it's grand. Come on.

*They exit hurriedly. Blackout. A slow dirge is heard. The creature's point of view is projected onto the screen, still the exterior of the building. The creature watches CIARÁN and SEÁN leave before sprinting off in an alternative direction. The music accelerates in tempo to match the pace of the creature. The projection fades with the music.*

*End of Act One.*

# ACT TWO

## Scene One

*The creature's point of view is projected onto the screen. We see a shack, surrounded by trees. The lights are raised to reveal the shack's interior. A single table centre-stage, two dusty armchairs, an old cupboard. There is a calendar attached to the wall upstage, above a fireplace, marked with occasional red crosses in a felt-tipped pen. Next to this is a glass window, a dim light spilling into the shack. CIARÁN is slumped on the sofa, motionless. He appears to be dead. There is a long pause before he wakes with a start. He looks around anxiously and composes himself from what was evidently some kind of nightmare. He stands and walks to the calendar. He finds the pen and marks another cross. On the projection, we see SEÁN approaching the shack. He pauses and looks back in the direction of the creature, having heard its movement. The creature retreats behind a tree, before peeping around to see SEÁN enter the shack. Simultaneously, he enters on stage and the projection fades. CIARÁN, engrossed in counting the crosses on the calendar, does not notice SEÁN's presence.*

**Seán**  'Bout ye, Ciarán.

*CIARÁN jumps.*

**Ciarán**  Christ Seán, what did I tell you? We had an arrangement, remember? Identify yourself the very second you enter, in that same moment. Shout my name, or your name, anything so I'll hear your voice. You'll get me all panicky again.

**Seán**  I thought you'd hear the door.

**Ciarán**  Well I didn't.

*SEÁN sits down.*

**Seán**  What have you been up to today? Back on the
Braille?

**Ciarán**  Thinking.

**Seán**  Thinking about what?

**Ciarán**  Nothing in particular.

**Seán**  Did you sleep last night?

**Ciarán**  For a wee while. Do I look as rough as I feel?

**Seán**  Just about. (*Pause.*) Another cross then.

**Ciarán**  Aye, well.

**Seán**  Just now?

**Ciarán**  Aye. I nodded off. And he's more defined this
time. I could make out every feature. That's eight times
already this month. What does he want?

**Seán**  He doesn't want anything. He doesn't exist.

**Ciarán**  Still in denial, Seán.

**Seán**  You're dreaming of the Grim Reaper. You've given
him a face. And a personality. It's daft.

**Ciarán**  His ears were bleeding.

**Seán**  Whose?

**Ciarán**  Death. His ears were bleeding this time. He didn't
seem to mind.

**Seán**  Then I don't see why you should.

**Ciarán**  And he's talking to me now, so he is.

**Seán**  What does he say?

**Ciarán**  I don't remember.

*CIARÁN looks at the calendar.*

But they're getting closer together. Like a countdown or something. Soon there'll be a red cross every other day. What are they counting down to?

**Seán**  Are you making tea, Ciarán?

**Ciarán**  I don't make tea anymore. You know that.

**Seán**  Right enough. I forgot.

*SEÁN stands and begins to make tea. CIARÁN slumps into a chair.*

**Ciarán**  I'm feeling crushed here.

**Seán**  What do you mean by that now?

**Ciarán**  I'm just so conscious that all we're doing is getting older, gradually fading. You know that pain in my kidneys has come back again? And my psoriasis is getting more severe. I feel as though I'm falling apart. Like the Grim Reaper is taking me in instalments.

**Seán**  You're getting worse.

**Ciarán**  Then let's go. Let's leave before something terrible happens.

**Seán**  How can we? When you're refusing to take even one step out of this place?

**Ciarán**  We're running out of time.

**Seán**  What are you saying?

**Ciarán**  It's these dreams about Death. I won't believe they're meaningless.

**Seán**  All they mean is that you're fucked in the head.

**Ciarán**  You said we'd be better off here.

**Seán**  You should be grateful. We're in the Republic. Unoccupied soil.

**Ciarán**  Don't you be starting on that talk now, Seán. You forget, no one cares about politics here.

**Seán**  Don't talk shite.

**Ciarán**  I'm serious. You talk about the troubles to the locals here, you'll find the subject changed soon enough. What will you do then? You'll have to survive on small talk. Not your strongest feature.

**Seán**  I can talk about other things, you know.

**Ciarán**  I haven't seen much evidence of that.

**Seán**  Fuck up.

**Ciarán**  I'm surprised you even brought us as far as Donegal. Believe it or not there are places on this planet where no one's ever even heard of Patrick Pearse, or Bobby Sands, or Wolfe Tone, or any of thems. You like living in your wee box, don't you?

**Seán**  It's important to me. It's important to a hell of a lot of people. Don't try and play it down. That's unfair. People have died for you.

**Ciarán**  I didn't ask anyone to die for me.

**Seán**  Aye, and that says more about you than it does about them. There's been a fire in this country of ours, Ciarán, and it's been raging on for years. You can't ignore it.

**Ciarán**  How could I? It's been feeding on the likes of us.

*There is a pause. This rings true to SEÁN.*

**Seán**  (*A change of tone.*) Here, do you want a wee cup of tea?

**Ciarán**  No, I'm grand.

*CIARÁN walks upstage, pensive. SEÁN begins to boil the kettle.*

Seven.

**Seán**  Seven what?

**Ciarán**  Archangels. There are seven archangels. (*Counting on fingers.*) Uriel, Raphael…

**Seán**  What are you doing?

**Ciarán**  Counting the archangels.

**Seán**  I know that. Why?

**Ciarán**  I'm learning angelology. (*Counting on fingers again.*) Uriel, Raphael, Raguel, Michael, Sariel, Gabriel, Remiel.

**Seán**  (*Exasperated.*) For fuck's sake.

**Ciarán**  They're God's warriors. Archangels, that is. They're on the second level of angelic hierarchy, just above your regular angels.

**Seán**  How many levels are there?

**Ciarán**  Nine.

**Seán**  What's the eighth?

**Ciarán**  Cherubim. Don't test me.

**Seán**  Ninth?

**Ciarán**  Seraphim. Don't test me. Don't test me.

**Seán**  Don't answer then.

**Ciarán**  Why are you always getting on at me?

**Seán**  I'm not getting on at you. You're paranoid, that's all. I mean more so than usual. I've never seen you this way. These dreams of Death 'n' all aren't helping matters. You're convinced they mean something, but they're only dreams, nothing more.

**Ciarán**  I told you. These aren't dreams, they're visitations.

*SEÁN begins to pour himself a cup of tea.*

I think I'll have that tea after all.

**Seán**  I want this behaviour to stop. It's not healthy. So I'll not be seeing any more red crosses on this calendar. Is that clear?

**Ciarán**  Two sugars please.

*SEÁN throws him a disapproving glance, and pours another cup.*

**Seán**  I'm really worried about you, so I am. You need to get out more.

**Ciarán**  They'll get me if I leave.

**Seán**  They don't know where we are. Sure if they did we'd be dead by now.

**Ciarán**  You're in my dreams as well.

**Seán**  Am I?

**Ciarán**  Aye. You keep trying to shake Death by the hand, but he isn't interested. You think you know him. But you don't.

*SEÁN hands CIARÁN the cup of tea.*

**Seán**  Here. Drink this. Slowly.

**Ciarán**  Why slowly?

**Seán**  So that your mouth can be occupied for as long as possible.

**Ciarán**  What's that supposed to mean?

**Seán**  You're ranting. And I'm getting a headache.

*CIARÁN takes a small bag of sweets out of his pocket.*

**Ciarán**  Would you like a cough drop?

**Seán**  I said I've got a headache, not a sore throat.

**Ciarán**  I thought you might enjoy the flavour.

*A beat.*

**Seán**  What flavour?

**Ciarán**  Blackcurrant.

**Seán**  Go on then.

*He takes one.*

**Ciarán**  (*To himself.*) Fifteen eighty-two. Ursula Kempe is tried as a witch at St Osyth in England and admits to keeping some astonishing pets. Listed as, item, four imps, item, two hecats named Titty and Jack, item, a black lamb called Tyffin, item, one toad called Piggish.

**Seán**  For God's sake.

**Ciarán**  No. Not Piggish. Pigin. Pig. In.

**Seán**  What's that got to do with angelology?

**Ciarán**  Nothing. Demonology. The flipside.

**Seán**  Forget about the flipside. It's not very Catholic of you to be so fixated with the occult. Either that or it's too Catholic. Either way, you'd be better off with your Braille.

**Ciarán**  Asmodeus: demon of lust. Aesma: demon of the Parsees. Shabriri: demon of ear diseases.

**Seán**  Stop that. Stop listing demons.

**Ciarán**  Orobas: Grand Prince of Hell. Xaphan: fans the furnaces of the underworld. Ronwe: gave us the knowledge of languages. Ukobach: invented fried food. Amduscias: gives concerts on the trumpet. Thanatos…

**Seán**  Enough, Ciarán.

**Ciarán**  Thanatos… I can't remember what Thanatos does.

**Seán**  How's the tea?

**Ciarán**  Not enough sugar.

**Seán**  I put two teaspoons in.

**Ciarán**  Not enough.

**Seán**  Give it here.

*He takes the cup and adds five more sugars.*

God love you. Sometimes I despair, I really do.

*He gives CIARÁN the cup.*

**Ciarán**  Thanks.

**Seán**  No bother.

*CIARÁN takes a sip.*

Better?

**Ciarán**  Slightly.

*SEÁN puts his coat on.*

What are you doing?

**Seán**  I'm putting my coat on.

**Ciarán**  I can see that. Why?

**Seán**  You'll be grand, Ciarán. I won't be long. You can come with me if you like.

**Ciarán**  You know I can't.

**Seán**  Well that's up to yourself.

**Ciarán**  I hate it when you go out. My imagination runs to all kinds of horror. I see your body, torn and splayed and left for scavengers.

*SEÁN is secretly disturbed by the image.*

**Seán**  Stop it. What's the matter with you?

**Ciarán**  Maybe I'm obsessed.

**Seán**  Aye, maybe you are.

**Ciarán**  When will you be back?

**Seán**  I can't say for sure. Some time tomorrow maybe.

**Ciarán**  Tomorrow? For God's sake Seán, where is it you're going?

**Seán**  Derry.

*There is a brief silence as CIARÁN takes this in.*

**Ciarán**  What are you saying? You can't go back to Derry, they'll fucking lynch you.

**Seán**  They won't.

**Ciarán**  Jesus, Seán. Derry's crawling with Provos, or friends of Provos, or friends of friends of Provos. You know that.

**Seán**  I'm going to talk to Malachy.

**Ciarán**  No. You can't. You know what'll happen.

**Seán**  You can't be so sure.

**Ciarán**  What are you at? You'll be up in front of the nutting squad before you can say *tiocfaidh ár lá.*

**Seán**  We're running out of options.

**Ciarán**  I thought you said we could stay here.

**Seán**  Aye, but for how long? I need to sort this thing out.

**Ciarán**  Malachy won't listen.

**Seán**  He's one of us. We've got a history. He was there when Da died, remember? These thing matter.

**Ciarán**  To fuck with him. My Da wouldn't have even been on that operation if it weren't for Malachy.

**Seán**  You don't know.

**Ciarán**  What don't I know?

**Seán**  Listen to me. Listen carefully. I'll be honest with you, we're not entirely safe here. This place isn't exactly our wee secret. People know about it.

**Ciarán**  Like who?

**Seán**  People. You know. The family.

**Ciarán**  What are you getting at?

**Seán**  The point is that if the Provos really want to find out where we are there are ways they can do that. There are people they can talk to. Who do you think owns this place?

**Ciarán**  Well, us. All of us. The Dohertys.

**Seán**  Aye, but who specifically?

**Ciarán**  I… I don't know.

**Seán**  You've got to remember there's money in these aul' cottages. If it wasn't so out of the way it'd be worth a fortune.

**Ciarán**  That's bollocks. Sure it's a total dive. It's practically derelict.

**Seán**  All I'm saying is we've got to be careful. We can't assume we can trust anyone.

**Ciarán**  Are you saying we'd be sold out by one of our own? By the family? (*A pause, then agitated.*) Is that what you're saying?

**Seán**  Ach, I don't know what I'm saying. Just thinking aloud is all.

**Ciarán**  Well don't.

**Seán**  You remember when Stevie Hughes was shot for touting? His own mother didn't go to his funeral. His own mother.

**Ciarán**  And do you think that's fair?

**Seán**  Don't know. She got a cassette tape the day after they done him. He'd confessed it all. Working for the peelers, giving up names, the lot.

**Ciarán**  I dunno, Sean. You put a gun to my head I'll tell you pretty much anything you want to hear.

**Seán**  They don't take these decisions lightly.

**Ciarán**  Well, that depends who's pulling the trigger, doesn't it?

**Seán**  He was guilty, no real doubt about that. But even so. His own mother. That's hard.

**Ciarán**  It is that.

**Seán**  See that's the way it is with families like ours, Ciarán. And it'll be the same with us. We've let the boys down. We've done a runner. In their eyes we've changed. We've turned. I'm your only family now.

**Ciarán**  Sweet Jesus, there's a thought.

**Seán**  I'll go and I'll speak to Malachy. And maybe I can sort this out.

**Ciarán**  You can't do that. I won't be able to bear it.

**Seán**  I haven't got a choice.

**Ciarán**  Maybe there's other places we can go. There's always a way if you just stop and think about it. You going to see Malachy is just about the most absurd idea I've ever heard. The hunted seeking out the hunter. You've got to be off your head.

*There is a pause. SEÁN seems pensive.*

**Seán** There's another reason. A better reason.

**Ciarán** What?

**Seán** (*Pause.*) Oh, fuck me.

*SEÁN sits down and covers his eyes. He seems frustrated, but not angry. He leans back and looks at CIARÁN.*

I'm going to have to go back to Derry, you know.

**Ciarán** No, Seán. I've told you. You can't do that to me.

*SEÁN's manner of speech becomes somewhat calmer, without being overly patronising.*

**Seán** It's not up for debate. As I say, I need to go back. There's no rush but.

*SEÁN takes his coat off. He walks over to the sideboard and takes out a bottle of Bushmills whiskey.*

**Ciarán** Where'd you get that?

**Seán** I got it from the village. The other day when you were napping. I know you like your Bush.

**Ciarán** (*Genuinely pleased.*) Happy days. I thought you said we couldn't afford it.

**Seán** We can't at the moment. But we will soon enough.

**Ciarán** How do you mean?

**Seán** (*Smiling.*) Just have a fucking drink would you?

*He sits next to CIARÁN and pours out two glasses of whiskey.*

**Ciarán** I do go on, don't I?

**Seán**  Aye, you do. But it's grand. It's just your nature.

**Ciarán**  This doesn't sound like you, Seán.

**Seán**  (*Ignoring this last remark.*) Here's what we'll do. I'll stay here with you for a while. We'll have a wee drink. We'll have a wee chat. And then you'll understand.

**Ciarán**  What is there to understand?

**Seán**  Don't rush me now. And don't worry. I'm telling you that I need to go back to the Bogside. I'm also telling you that I don't need to go right away. So there's no need for you to get upset.

**Ciarán**  I don't understand you.

**Seán**  I don't suppose I understand you either. Doesn't matter. You're my wee brother. That's enough for me.

*CIARÁN takes a sip of whiskey.*

**Ciarán**  That's dead on.

**Seán**  Aye. (*Examining the whiskey bottle.*) Bushmills. Great whiskey. Shitty town.

**Ciarán**  It is that.

**Seán**  Can't move for all the fucking huns.

**Ciarán**  Now don't be starting on about all that.

**Seán**  Ach, I'm kidding. Winding you up.

*They both take another sip. SEÁN looks around the room.*

Our great-grandfather was born here, did you know that?

**Ciarán**  In Donegal?

**Seán**  No. Here. In this room. Or so I've been told.

**Ciarán**  I thought he was a Dubliner.

**Seán**  No. He went there to join the IRB. Got caught up in the movement. You know all this.

**Ciarán**  Aye. Survived the rising. Died at the Four Courts. I've heard it all before.

**Seán**  Funny to think, though. This is where he started, all those years ago. Kicking and screaming. Right here.

*SEÁN looks around, trying to locate a memory.*

I remember you used to get so excited about coming out here.

**Ciarán**  Really? I don't. I remember getting splinters from that sideboard, that's what I remember. And that year we got so sunburnt we couldn't sleep for the pain.

**Seán**  You've a selective memory. We'd come out here every summer to get away from the troubles 'n' all. And you'd keep going on at me, asking when we were going, and how much longer we had to wait, and all of that. It's funny. You've always been a whinger, but I think I used to find it endearing.

**Ciarán**  What changed your mind?

**Seán**  Well when Ma died it was just myself bearing the brunt of it. That's a lot to take for an eighteen year-old. Christ, it's a lot to take for anyone.

*SEÁN takes another sip of whiskey.*

Sometimes I think about that night they took her. She'd been running down Foyle Road, punching the windows of houses as she passed them. A few of them broke. That's why she was so badly cut. And she'd been screaming at everyone she saw.

**Ciarán**  Screaming what?

**Seán**  Nothing. No words. Just constant screams, like she'd seen something awful and she couldn't shake it off. This was my mother. This deranged creature – and she did look like a creature – this thing who'd been wrestled to the floor, her face and fists cut to ribbons. This was the woman who gave me life. That was a feeling I didn't particularly care for.

*CIARÁN looks away.*

And it made me not want to help her, do you see what I mean? They came in from next door, and Doctor Brennan and all of them'ens. And she had this stick between her teeth, and she kept pushing at the air. Just pushing it, like she was trying to drive away some kind of invisible enemy. She was exhausted by the time you got back.

**Ciarán** You should have let me see her.

**Seán** No. You couldn't have seen her. You were too young.

**Ciarán** I had a right to see her. You know that.

**Seán** Why should you have that right? I was protecting you. I've always been protecting you. You've no right at all to tell me how I should be doing it. You're being ungrateful, so you are.

**Ciarán** I'm not ungrateful, Seán. I just wish… I just wanted to see her is all.

**Seán** Listen to me, Ciarán. When people die young that's how you remember them. Good looking, full of energy. It's the final image that sticks. Let me ask you this. How do you remember Ma?

**Ciarán** I don't remember much. But I can see her face. I can see that she loved me. And she had a look in her eyes. Utter devotion, so it was.

**Seán** Aye. But when they took her she was a different woman. She looked, chaotic. In a frenzy. You know, her hair all over the place, eyes bloodshot and seeping. Christ almighty, she was in a wile state.

**Ciarán**  Did she say anything?

**Seán**  She made noises, she didn't speak. (*Pause.*) She knew what was happening to herself, do you know that?

**Ciarán**  How can you be sure?

**Seán**  Because she told me. That was the worst thing about it. She understood it all. In her clearer moments she was terrified of what would happen. And most of all, what would happen to you.

**Ciarán**  To me?

**Seán**  Aye. She was scared stiff. And she made me promise.

**Ciarán**  Promise what?

*There is a pause.*

**Seán**  That I wouldn't let them have you.

*Another pause.*

**Ciarán**  I remember there were moments. Like I'd catch her staring into space for no reason at all, tapping the knife edge against her wrists. And I remember being scared of her. Just sometimes, like. Every now and then there'd be one of those moments, and I could see her mind was elsewhere, somewhere terrible. And you couldn't talk to her when she was like that. She couldn't speak at all.

*CIARÁN hesitates for a moment, a look of concern on his face.*

Seán, you don't think that maybe I've…

**Seán**  (*Interrupting.*) No.

**Ciarán**  No. (*Pause.*) No, of course not.

*CIARÁN looks down. SEÁN looks at him for a moment, before standing and putting his coat back on.*

**Seán**  I'd best be off.

**Ciarán**  No, Seán. There's something you're wanting to tell me.

**Seán**  There's isn't.

**Ciarán**  No? Then in that case there's something you should be telling me.

**Seán**  That's enough for now.

**Ciarán**  For once Seán, just for once, don't treat me like a wean.

*SEÁN considers this for a moment before sitting down.*

**Seán**  You say you remember Ma. You remember that look of… What was it you said, devotion?

**Ciarán**  Aye.

**Seán**  Possibly. There was devotion in her for a while right enough. But there was fear there too, and that never went away. Fear that we'd end up just like all the other men in our family. Sacrificed for the sake of a united Ireland that never seemed to get any closer. She used to say it wasn't a cause at all, it was a curse. But the thing is, she didn't understand. She didn't understand how important it was to us. To me.

**Ciarán**  What is it you've got to say, Seán?

**Seán**  I've been telling you lies.

**Ciarán**  What do you mean?

**Seán**  About Malachy.

*SEÁN looks down. He doesn't want to tell.*

Oh, God.

**Ciarán**  What? What are you talking about?

**Seán**  Hang on there a wee second. Don't rush me. I… I owe you an explanation.

**Ciarán**  (*Impatient.*) About what? For Jesus' sake would you just spit it out?

**Seán**  Shut up, Ciarán. I'm not going to have this conversation with you if you don't calm down.

**Ciarán**  Okay. (*Pause.*) Okay, I'm calm.

**Seán**  Are you sure?

*CIARÁN is leaning forward, barely containing his frustration.*

**Ciarán**  Tell me what this is all about.

**Seán**  We have money. Lots of it.

*A long pause.*

**Ciarán**  What are you saying?

**Seán**  I'm not speaking in riddles, Ciarán.

**Ciarán**  How is it we have money? Look at where it is we're living.

**Seán**  Aye, but there's money back at the Bog. It's ours. It's our birthright. It was my Ma's.

**Ciarán**  I… I don't understand.

**Seán**  And what's more, it's been keeping us going for years.

**Ciarán**  Keeping us going how exactly? Why've you been slogging your guts out for Malachy if we've got money? You're not making any sense.

**Seán**  See when my Ma died she'd lost everything. She couldn't even recognise her own face in the mirror, for fuck's sake. But no matter what happened to her, she always knew her responsibilities. I can't take that away from her.

**Ciarán**  Explain to me Seán, 'cause I'm not sure where this is going exactly. Ma left us money?

**Seán**  Aye.

**Ciarán**  Lots of money?

**Seán**  Well, enough.

*SEÁN stands and paces around the room.*

I don't know if you'll want to hear this.

**Ciarán**  Just say it, for fuck's sake.

**Seán**  All this time, you think I've been getting backhanders from Malachy. It never happened. It's a lie.

**Ciarán**  (*Angry, but restrained.*) Go on.

**Seán**  He's never paid me a penny. And he's not been skimming off the 'RA. I've been working for the cause and for the cause alone, to help the boys. Ma's money's been there all along, I'd hidden it. That's why I've got to go back. We'll be needing it now more than ever.

**Ciarán**  Wait now. All these deliveries, all these covert fucking meetings, all that shite. What are you telling me, that you weren't getting paid?

**Seán**  That's exactly what I'm telling you.

**Ciarán**  So you've been doing this shit for all these years for nothing? For nothing at all? Jesus, that's desperate.

**Seán**  Not for nothing. For our family. For the cause. You can't possibly know what a difference I've made. Remember Bobby Sands. 'Everyone Republican or otherwise has his own particular part to play.' There's a truth to that, Ciarán.

**Ciarán**  We're not part of this. We were never supposed to be part of this. You said it yourself. Ma wanted it over and done with. There's a cycle in our family, and it needs to be broken.

**Seán**  Not until the job is done.

**Ciarán**  What's that supposed to mean?

**Seán**  I know you think I'm thick. Because I don't read as much as you, you think I've no idea what's going on. But I do think about history. And here's what it means to me. The Four Courts, Swatragh, the battle of the Bogside. These events mean something to our family. Like we've been chipping away at some almighty block of stone. Like we've all been contributing to that one vision, a perfect sculpture, a united Ireland. But we're not there yet. It's a job half done. Why should it matter how many generations of our family has to die, so long as we finish what we started all those years ago?

**Ciarán**  It's got nothing to do with us.

**Seán**  How can you sit there and say that? Have some self-respect.

**Ciarán**  Self-respect? You're the one who's been working as a fucking dogsbody. And look where you've ended up for it. That's gratitude, so it is.

**Seán**  You let that creature go, not me.

**Ciarán**  Don't you do that. I wouldn't have been in that situation in the first place if you weren't so desperate to join the 'RA.

**Seán**  I shouldn't have told you. I shouldn't have said a word.

**Ciarán**  You're not my father, Seán. I don't want your fucking protection anymore.

**Seán**  You'll obsess about this. I really shouldn't have told you.

**Ciarán**  If you really wanted all this why didn't you join them in the first place?

**Seán**  (*Shouts.*) I couldn't! (*A long pause.*) They wouldn't fucking have me.

*There is a long silence.*

**Ciarán**  So that's it. They wouldn't let you join but they'd let you be their puppy dog. Fetching, carrying, and all for the privilege of feeling like you're a volunteer. Do you know how pathetic that is?

**Seán**  Maybe. (*Pause, then defiant.*) But it hasn't been a waste.

**Ciarán**  Where's it got us? Hiding out in this fucking shack?

**Seán**  Ach, I'm away.

*SEÁN makes a move to the door. He stops and turns around.*

It hasn't been a waste, Ciarán. You'll see that eventually. (*Pause.*) I'll go back, get the money, and we'll be grand. And there'll be no regrets. Alright?

*CIARÁN does not respond.*

If we can get out of this then we'll never have to think about any of them bastards. We can forget all about it. And then we'll be well away from all this shite. Just like my Ma wanted in the first place. She can rest easy. (*Pause.*) And so can we. (*Pause.*) You'll be alright?

*CIARÁN remains silent. SEÁN picks up his mobile telephone.*

Here. I'll give you a wee ring when I'm on my way back.

*A pause. CIARÁN seems a mile away.*

Ciarán.

*A pause.*

Ciarán.

*CIARÁN looks up at SEÁN.*

**Ciarán**   You should have let me see her.

*SEÁN looks at CIARÁN for a while before he turns and exits. CIARÁN stands and paces very slowly over to the mirror. He gently reaches out a hand and touches his reflection. He seems almost catatonic. After a few moments he begins to cry uncontrollably, clearly getting something out of his system. He hits his own head and tries to regain control. Through the stuttering cries he tries to recite his demons.*

Orobas…the Grand High Prince. Xaphan, fans the… fans the furnaces of Hell. Ronwe…taught us languages… Ukobach, invented…fried…food. Amduscias plays the trumpet… Thanatos…

*He cannot remember.*

Thanatos… Thanatos.

*He runs over to the table and finds his book. He flicks to the correct page.*

Thanatos: Prince of Death.

*CIARÁN closes the book and glances around nervously. He puts the chain on the latch of the door.*

You just leave me alone.

*Blackout.*

# Scene Two

*Soft discordant music is heard. The creature's view is projected onto the screen; we see the exterior of the shack again. THE CLOCK is seen, walking towards the shack at a measured pace. He is a huge figure in a black balaclava, carrying a large hammer. The lights are raised on stage. CIARÁN is now sitting in one of the armchairs, reading from the book of demonology.*

**Ciarán**  Fallen angels.

*He covers the page with his hand to test himself. He looks up and recites. We see THE CLOCK approaching on the projection.*

Tabaet: son of the serpent. Penemue: instructed mankind how to write. Gadreel: led Eve astray and provided weapons for mankind. Jeqon: guided the other angels into limbo. Asbeel. Kasbeel. Kokabel. Turael.

*THE CLOCK's face appears at the window. The projection fades.*

Azazel. Batarjal. Hananel.

*He pauses to think. THE CLOCK leaves the window and heads for the front door.*

Tumael?

*He looks at the page.*

(*Correcting himself.*) Rumael. Fuck. All them bastards sound the same.

*There is a knock. CIARÁN stands and slowly makes his way over to the door. He stops half-way and considers it more carefully. Another knock, louder this time. CIARÁN takes a nervous pace forward then stops again.*

Seán? Is that you?

*Another knock.*

Seán, if that's you then please say something.

*Another knock, more insistent.*

This really isn't funny, Seán.

*Another knock. There is a pause.*

Seán?

*The knocking begins again, but this time it is sustained. CIARÁN hesitates for a second before unlatching the door. As he reaches out to the door handle, the knocking stops.*

I'm going to kick your arse, Seán.

*CIARÁN opens the door. He stands in the open doorway for a short while, looking out. There is a long, dangerous pause. The mobile telephone on the table suddenly rings. CIARÁN looks at the phone, and back to the door, uncertain what to do. He shuts the door and puts the chain back on the latch. He runs over to the phone and answers it.*

Hello? Seán, what the fuck's taking you so long? Shit Seán, someone's knocking at the fucking door. I opened it but there's no one there. No I didn't imagine it. (*Pause.*) Where are you? (*Pause.*) Well I may not be alive in another five minutes, so hurry the fuck up.

*There is an aggressive knock at the door.*

Shit, did you hear that? Christ Seán, tell me you've got a gun or something here. I can't calm down! There's a…

*Another knock.*

(*Panicking.*) Oh fuck me they've found us. That fucker Malachy's found us. Shit! What do I do? What do I do?

*The door splits open. We see the hammer penetrating the wood.*

(*Utter panic.*) They're breaking in, Seán! They'll fucking kill me. Why didn't we have a gun? You always wanted

81

a fucking gun! Well you shouldn't be fucking listening to me now, should you?

*THE CLOCK's arm is seen punching through the hole he has made in the door. He reaches round and unlocks it. He kicks the door open and steps inside. CIARÁN drops the phone and backs away, staring at him.*

Oh, God.

*THE CLOCK stares at CIARÁN. There is a pause. Slowly, THE CLOCK moves towards CIARÁN, who retreats at the same pace, until THE CLOCK is centre-stage. They both stop.*

Er…hello there.

*A beat. THE CLOCK does not move.*

Listen, I want you to know something. None of this was my fault. I've done nothing on you lads, I swear. And, and more importantly, and I must emphasise this, I will be willing to tell you absolutely anything you want to know. Really. You won't have to ask me twice. So. (*Pause.*) Won't you say anything?

*A long pause.*

You're in Malachy's company I suppose. Is there just the one of yous?

*CIARÁN looks around for show. He is desperately trying to buy time.*

You know I've always admired you lads. Anyone who'll stand up to them Orange wankers, or the fucking Brits. You know my cousin's best friend was shot by a soldier. She was banging her dustbin lid on the ground to warn everyone that the squaddies were coming, and the fucker shot her. He just shot her. That's British justice for you. Let their wee men with big guns make choices over life and death.

*THE CLOCK takes a step towards him.*

Listen now. I'll come straight to the point, because that's what, er, because you seem to… Well, the wee animal. What was that all about mate? Sure that's a wile peculiar way to be making your money, so it is. I suppose it was a wee bit more imaginative than robbing a bank, but sure it had us wile confused.

*THE CLOCK takes another step towards him. CIARÁN's manner of speech becomes more erratic.*

Will you not say anything to me? You're making me very nervous. (*An anxious smile.*) I suppose that's the point, isn't it? But see I'm not a tout, I'm not a Prod, I'm one of yous. You don't need to take me to your wee room and kick it out of me. I let the wee animal go, and I'm so sorry for it. But I'll make it up for yous. You go on and tell Malachy that. Why will you not speak? Will you please just say something?

*THE CLOCK advances another step.*

(*Holding out his hands.*) Wait! Please, there's really no need. Listen, think about this. Seán's done so much for you boys over the years. And…and I'm not saying you owe us or anything, but…sure he wasn't even getting paid for it.

*Another step.*

Now don't take that the wrong way. I… I was just saying is all. I know it's to get the Brits out, and I'm not saying we should've been paid. We're only too happy to do our bit for our country. Don't get me wrong.

*Another step.*

I've pissed you off, haven't I? I've said the wrong thing. Listen, we should wait for Seán, because he'll tell you. He'll know what to do about all this.

*Another step.*

(*In genuine desperation.*) No! No, don't do that.

*Another step. CIARÁN grabs a bottle and smashes it against THE CLOCK's face. He doesn't even flinch.*

Oh no.

*Another step. CIARÁN grabs the fire poker.*

Right now I don't want this. Just let me go and there'll be no trouble.

*THE CLOCK walks steadily towards him, ignoring his protests.*

No! No, don't do that! Please! I don't want to…

*He takes a feeble swing at THE CLOCK, who simply disarms CIARÁN before grabbing him by the neck and pushing him against the door.*

(*Crying.*) I'm, I'm, I'm really really sorry about that, I just. I er, panicked, you know? Obviously I wouldn't dare to hurt you, or try and hurt you, I…

*THE CLOCK pulls CIARÁN round and throws him with incredible force against the other side of the room. CIARÁN hits the wall and falls, groaning in pain. THE CLOCK begins to advance, and CIARÁN manages to scramble to his feet.*

Oh no, please. This isn't supposed to happen. We're supposed to be safe. You're not supposed to know we're here!

*CIARÁN tries to evade THE CLOCK by running around the room, behind the chair, pushing furniture in his path. THE CLOCK cannot be stopped. He advances towards CIARÁN, despite all his efforts, slowly and inevitably.*

Listen, this is all a huge misunderstanding. Please just call Malachy. You don't have to do this. I've done nothing wrong. I've done nothing on you boys. Jesus, what's the matter with you? Will you not just say one fucking word?

*THE CLOCK pulls CIARÁN to the floor centre-stage. He kicks him forcefully in the stomach. He then holds him in place, despite CIARÁN's struggling. He easily overpowers him, and clamps him to the floor with a single hand, CIARÁN still writhing to escape. THE CLOCK sits on CIARÁN, holding his arms to his side with his legs. CIARÁN kicks away redundantly as THE CLOCK prepares the hammer.*

(*Shouting now.*) Please don't hurt me! Let me speak to Malachy!

*THE CLOCK raises the hammer. SEÁN runs in and throws himself against his body. There is a violent struggle. THE CLOCK eventually pins SEÁN to the floor, and begins to throttle him. CIARÁN hits THE CLOCK on the back of the head with the fire poker, rendering him unconscious. THE CLOCK slumps forward onto SEÁN. There is a pause.*

**Seán** Ciarán?

*CIARÁN does not respond. He is evidently in a state of shock.*

Ciarán! Will you get this fat fucker off me?

**Ciarán** Right. Sorry.

*With a combined effort, they roll THE CLOCK away.*

**Seán** I thought you were a pacifist.

**Ciarán** I am.

**Seán** Well for a pacifist you're pretty mean with the poker.

**Ciarán** I didn't hit him that hard.

**Seán**  Well it wasn't exactly a light slap on the wrist.

*SEÁN feels for his pulse.*

He's dead.

**Ciarán**  What?

**Seán**  Ach, I'm joking. He's just unconscious. He's lucky but. There's not too many lads out there could survive a knock like that.

**Ciarán**  I told you. It wasn't all that hard.

*SEÁN feels THE CLOCK's head.*

**Seán**  Well there's a definite lump.

**Ciarán**  That doesn't prove anything. Some people just have lumpy heads.

**Seán**  Here, put him on this chair.

*They do so with some difficulty.*

(*Pause, then diffidently.*) Are you alright?

**Ciarán**  (*Sarcastic.*) I'm dead on. Never been better.

**Seán**  Okay. Okay.

**Ciarán**  What took you so long? When you phoned you said you were only a minute away.

**Seán**  Shut up would you? It was bad enough having to sprint here and wrestle this bastard off you, without having to put up with your whinging. I'm knackered. And here.

*He passes the bag to CIARÁN, who looks inside. SEÁN closes the now damaged door.*

**Ciarán**  You found it.

**Seán**  Aye. It's all there.

**Ciarán**  Thank Christ for that.

**Seán**  It means we can leave. We can get out of this dump at last.

*CIARÁN points at THE CLOCK.*

**Ciarán**  This presents a slight complication.

**Seán**  You're right. (*Pause.*) We'd better tie him up.

**Ciarán**  He's out cold, mind.

**Seán**  Aye, but I'm taking no chances. Have we got anything we can use? Any rope or twine or something?

**Ciarán**  I'll see what I can find.

*CIARÁN exits. SEÁN squats down next to THE CLOCK and looks at him.*

**Seán**  (*Calling to CIARÁN.*) Just the one of them?

**Ciarán**  (*Off.*) Aye! Weird, isn't it?

**Seán**  (*To himself.*) Aye. It is that.

*There is a short pause, before he slowly reaches a hand up and starts to pull the balaclava off the head of THE CLOCK. CIARÁN enters as he does so, carrying a length of rope.*

**Ciarán**  Seán I found this in your… What are you doing?

*SEÁN stops pulling on the balaclava, and stands.*

**Seán**  I was just going to take his mask off. I want to see his face.

**Ciarán**  Why? To give the IRA another reason to kill you?

**Seán**  (*Sarcastic.*) That's right, Ciarán. I just wanted to make absolutely sure they'd go through with it.

**Ciarán**  Leave the balaclava on. I don't want to see him.

**Seán** Why? They're going to do us both, whether we've seen his face or not.

*He tries to pull the balaclava off again. CIARÁN grabs his hands to prevent him.*

**Ciarán** Would you give it a fucking rest?

**Seán** Oh come on. It'll be someone we know. Did his voice sound familiar?

**Ciarán** He didn't say anything. Not a word. That was the worst thing about it.

**Seán** What?

**Ciarán** I just couldn't bear it. The silence. I don't know why. It just felt so wrong. Like I was losing my mind or something. But please, I can't see his face. I just can't. It's nothing to do with identification or any of that shite. I just…don't want to see him. There's something at the back of my mind. Something about this fella. It's familiar.

**Seán** What are you talking about?

**Ciarán** Just please, please don't take his mask off.

**Seán** I didn't want you to open Malachy's box, but you still did. And look where that got us.

*CIARÁN pulls SEÁN closer to him, looking into his eyes.*

**Ciarán** (*Slowly and emphatically.*) Exactly.

*There is a pause. SEÁN pulls his hands away roughly.*

**Seán** Give me the rope.

*CIARÁN does so. SEÁN ties THE CLOCK's hands behind his back, then walks upstage.*

**Ciarán** So what do we do with him?

**Seán**  Let me think about it.

**Ciarán**  We'd better make a decision right enough. He could come round any time.

**Seán**  He's out cold, Ciarán. And he's tied up. I did a double knot.

**Ciarán**  A double knot? I didn't realise it was a double knot. We're grand, then.

**Seán**  None of your lip.

**Ciarán**  So now what?

**Seán**  Now I think I could do with a wee sandwich.

**Ciarán**  We're out of cheese.

**Seán**  We're always out of cheese. I'll improvise. We can have something to eat, then we'll decide what to do.

*SEÁN exits. CIARÁN stares at THE CLOCK.*

**Ciarán**  (*Shouting to SEÁN.*) Why do you think he's not got a gun?

**Seán**  (*Off.*) Dunno. Strange through. Bacon do you?

**Ciarán**  Aye. (*Pause.*) Why would he be alone? How many in a punishment squad?

**Seán**  (*Off.*) Varies. Usually three or four. The bacon's cold but.

**Ciarán**  It's grand.

*He steps towards THE CLOCK and kneels, eyeing him suspiciously.*

(*To himself.*) Belial. Demon of hypocrisy. Beyrevra. Indian demon. Pulled off one of the five heads of Brahma.

**Seán**  (*Off.*) You want tomato?

**Ciarán** Just a wee bit!

*He edges closer to THE CLOCK.*

Harangal. Brings health to the sick, rolls like a wheel, in charge of fifty legions. Beelzebub. Witches kiss his footprints, when summoned appears in the form of a...

*He edges closer, now almost face to face with THE CLOCK.*

Huge fly.

*He calls again to SEÁN.*

Seán, there's something in his pocket!

**Seán** (*Off.*) Is it a gun?

**Ciarán** (*Calling.*) Just a second!

*CIARÁN gingerly reaches for THE CLOCK's pocket and pulls out a small alarm clock. He examines it carefully, somewhat baffled. THE CLOCK suddenly grabs CIARÁN's hair and throws him to the floor. He winds the rope that was binding his hands around CIARÁN's neck and begins to pull. CIARÁN manages to scream SEÁN's name. SEÁN enters and lunges at THE CLOCK. After a brief struggle THE CLOCK is rendered unconscious again by another strike to the head.*

**Seán** Did you fucking untie him?

**Ciarán** Of course I didn't untie him. He must've loosened the rope.

**Seán** How? How could he have done that?

**Ciarán** Quick, before he comes round again.

*They tie him up again.*

Where was it you learnt that double knot?

**Seán** Not another word.

**Ciarán**  It's a clock, Seán. Like in the paper. The man in the mask who cripples his victims.

*SEÁN takes the clock from him.*

**Seán**  Where's you get this?

**Ciarán**  It was in his pocket. It's him. It's your man from the papers. He's not a Provo. The Provos would have burst in here *en masse*, waving their guns and ranting about how we'd jeopardised the cause. This one comes here alone, armed with a hammer, and he won't say a single word. If you hadn't returned I'd be watching the countdown to my own death on that wee clock there, my legs mashed to a pulp.

**Seán**  Okay, okay. Calm down there a wee second.

**Ciarán**  What are you thinking?

**Seán**  Just a minute.

*There is a pause.*

**Ciarán**  Seán?

**Seán**  (*Agitated.*) What?

**Ciarán**  What are you thinking?

**Seán**  I… I'm not sure. Just give me a moment.

*He sits down.*

**Ciarán**  We should call the police.

**Seán**  No. I've never called on the RUC in my life, and I'm not about to start now.

**Ciarán**  We're over the border, remember? It'll be the Gardai.

**Seán**  Same difference. They won't want to touch this one. They'll leave it to the peelers in the north. Or maybe the army.

**Ciarán**  But Seán…

**Seán**  We're leaving the security forces out of this.

**Ciarán**  For Christ's sake, this isn't about the dominance of the Orange State. This is something else. It's entirely unrelated. You're being irrational.

**Seán**  No, irrational is breaking down people's doors in the middle of the night and arresting boys without trial. Irrational is gunning down thirteen unarmed civilians at a civil rights march and claiming that it wasn't murder. Don't you talk to me about irrational, Ciarán. I grew up in Derry. I've no right to be rational.

**Ciarán**  (*Getting worked up.*) This isn't about you or me, or the Republicans or the Loyalists. This is about a lunatic who needs to be locked away.

**Seán**  I'm not calling on the RUC.

**Ciarán**  So what then? You can't go running to the Provos anymore.

**Seán**  (*A sudden thought.*) What about Brendan Flannery? Or Colm O'Connell? This man's guilty of killing Republican volunteers. Maybe we can strike a deal with Malachy. We could get immunity if we hand him over.

**Ciarán**  They want us dead. If we hand him over they'll kill the three of us. Forgiveness isn't in their nature.

**Seán**  Well, we'll have to think of something.

*SEÁN stands and takes a few steps, pensive.*

**Ciarán**  Something's just occurred to me.

**Seán**  What?

**Ciarán**  I dreamt this.

**Seán**  Oh Christ. I don't know if I can bear anymore of your dreams.

**Ciarán**  No, listen. There's something about the way you're standing. And the chair. (*Pointing to the alarm clock.*) And your man here. It's familiar.

**Seán**  It's just déjà vu. Don't make such a big deal out of it.

**Ciarán**  But I… (*He thinks for a second.*) I remember something else. Oh God.

**Seán**  Do you want to tell me what all this shite is about?

**Ciarán**  It's just that… He's the one from my dream.

**Seán**  Who? (*Indicating THE CLOCK.*) Him?

**Ciarán**  Aye. It's Death, so it is.

**Seán**  What is? What are you talking about?

**Ciarán**  Your man here. He's Death, so he is. He's the one I've been dreaming about. I just know it.

**Seán**  Catch yourself on.

**Ciarán**  He's the right build. What if it is him? What if this is Death himself? I couldn't bear it.

**Seán**  It's not Death, Ciarán. It's a fat psychopath.

**Ciarán**  (*Insistent.*) But what if?

**Seán**  I can't have this discussion anymore. It's absurd. Underneath this mask is either an IRA volunteer on an assignment from Malachy to bring us in, or a widely-publicised serial killer. It is not the personification of Death as previewed in Mr Ciarán Doherty's recurring nightmares.

**Ciarán**  Maybe they're one and the same.

**Seán**  What?

**Ciarán**  It makes perfect sense. A mysterious figure roams around the country. He can't be caught. He can't be hurt. He just kills, without regard for age, gender, or religion. He floats from victim to victim, faceless like a plague, and the press christen him 'The Clock'. But that's it, you see. There's nothing new in that. It's just the Grim Reaper all over again.

**Seán** (*Contemptuously.*) I see. Instead of a scythe he has a hammer.

**Ciarán** Exactly.

**Seán** You're talking shit again.

**Ciarán** I'm not, I promise you. I'm remembering this. And it's not déjà vu. It's more defined than that. (*Indicates THE CLOCK.*) I've seen his face before. I know what's underneath that mask.

**Seán** That's enough now. You're wasting my time.

**Ciarán** And he's…he's…

**Seán** (*Very impatient.*) He's what?

**Ciarán** Well I… I don't know if I should tell you.

**Seán** Tell me what?

**Ciarán** He's come for you.

**Seán** What's that supposed to mean?

**Ciarán** He's chosen you. He's been watching you for a while now. And all of a sudden it's time, and there's nothing you can do to stop it.

*SEÁN seems uneasy.*

**Seán** Just stop it, will you? You're freaking me out here.

**Ciarán** He's found you just like he found Colm O'Connell. (*A sudden recollection.*) Wait, wait. I'm remembering it now. All of it. (*Points.*) You are standing there. And you want to see his face. So you take off his mask. And that's when he gets you. That's when he strikes.

**Seán**  Well, you're not to worry. I didn't take it off, did I?

**Ciarán**  (*Ominously.*) Not yet.

**Seán**  I'm not going to take it off. Alright?

**Ciarán**  But you will. And when you do take it off, you'll look straight into his face. And he'll smile at you. (*Terrified.*) I've seen it. I've seen that face. I can even describe it to you.

**Seán**  Well, don't bother yourself. I don't want to hear any more of this shit.

**Ciarán**  We have to call the police. We just have to.

**Seán**  Fuck up. It's out of the question.

**Ciarán**  We've got no choice.

**Seán**  Ciarán, if you don't stop talking this way I'll slap you till you bleed.

*There is a long pause.*

We'll just have to kill him.

**Ciarán**  (*Pause.*) What are you talking about? You can't kill Death. He's like a mist or something. I hit him with that bottle, but it just sailed straight through him. He's invincible.

**Seán**  He's not invincible, Ciarán.

**Ciarán**  Let's just take our money and get out of here. We can make a fresh start.

**Seán**  Think about it. Yes, we could leave. Forget all about this. But if we don't kill him he'll just carry on doing his thing. And see every time you read about another murder you'll know we could have prevented it. You want that kind of responsibility?

**Ciarán**  It doesn't matter anyway. We're not killers.

**Seán**  (*Pause.*) Give me the hammer.

**Ciarán**  What?

**Seán**  Come on now. The hammer. Hurry up.

**Ciarán**  You're not going to do this, Seán, so you can stop pretending.

**Seán**  You think you know me so well, don't you?

**Ciarán**  Aye, I do. And you know I'm right, so stop mucking about.

*SEÁN picks the hammer up himself, eyeing CIARÁN all the while. He stands next to THE CLOCK and holds the hammer to his head. He pulls it back, preparing to strike.*

**Seán**  You really want to see this?

**Ciarán**  (*Smiling.*) Absolutely. You go on. You pummel the bastard to a pulp.

**Seán**  I'll do it, you know.

**Ciarán**  Sure you will.

**Seán**  I mean it.

**Ciarán**  Seán, this is a game you cannot win. I've sussed you out. You're waiting for me to stop you, to raise any kind of objection so that I'm the coward and you're still the hero. But for once I'm not going to do it.

**Seán**  (*Slowly, a kind of warning.*) I will do this thing.

**Ciarán**  No you won't. If I don't stop you it'll be a simple choice. Your stupid pride or this man's life. (*Pause.*) But whoever, or whatever he is, it doesn't matter. You're not any kind of killer.

**Seán**  You're really so confident that you're prepared to gamble his life?

**Ciarán**  There's no gamble. You're my brother. I know you about as well as any man can know another. You've always tried to pretend that we have nothing in common. But this here's the truth, like it or no. I know you won't kill him, because I wouldn't kill him.

**Seán**  (*Pause.*) It's a dangerous game but.

**Ciarán**  Do it. Bash in his skull.

*There is a pause. The creature's view is projected onto the screen. It is approaching the shack, slowly. SEÁN looks alternately at THE CLOCK and CIARÁN, still holding the hammer aloft. The creature reaches the door and the projection fades. He throws the hammer to the floor and storms upstage.*

**Seán**  Don't you fucking say a word.

**Ciarán**  I wasn't going to.

**Seán**  I swear to God, if you start gloating, I'll never forgive you.

**Ciarán**  Gloating? This isn't one-upmanship. The reason I didn't stop you is because I wanted you to admit it to yourself.

**Seán**  Admit what?

**Ciarán**  That you're not, and never will be, a killer. That you flirt with criminals and terrorists and that whole darker side of life, but you're always at the borders. You're always in the half-light.

**Seán**  We don't need to kill him. He's tied up and unconscious. There are other options.

**Ciarán**  Why can't you just admit that you're not capable of murder? However much you want to live up to Da's expectations, you're our mother through and through. You know that.

**Seán**  I could kill. I'd kill for my country.

**Ciarán**  You always say that Seán, but you never could.

**Seán**  Well I did kill a man, Ciarán. So fuck you.

*SEÁN walks to the other side of the room and pours himself a drink.*

**Ciarán**  (*Not really believing him.*) Oh really? Who did you kill then? Let me guess. You suffocated some poor Orangeman with his own bowler hat?

**Seán**  He was in the RUC.

**Ciarán**  (*Pause.*) I almost think you're serious.

**Seán**  I am serious.

**Ciarán**  I'm not in the mood for this. You shouldn't joke about death.

**Seán**  I told you. I'm serious.

**Ciarán**  You killed a man? An RUC man?

**Seán**  Well. RUC by day, UVF by night. You know the sort. They were all at it. And you tell me there's never been any real collusion between the state and the loyalists. You call it nationalist paranoia. You call it IRA rhetoric. Well maybe it is some of the time. And maybe it isn't. But when your man comes home from work of an evening, and replaces his policeman's cap with a balaclava, is he likely to respect the privacy of his suspects? Names. Addresses. Family details. Where he goes to work. Where he likes to shop. Who he likes to fuck. His entire fucking routine. And the RUC hold up their hands and plead ignorance. But ask yourself this. Even if some of them are telling the truth, and they know fuck all about it, how many RUC men would shed a tear for a few dead Provos?

**Ciarán**  It's not the RUC anymore. It's the PSNI.

**Seán** (*In a rage.*) You're a fucking pedantic bastard, so you are! It's the same fucking animal, don't you know that? They change the name, they change the uniform, they take down the Union Jack from their stations, but it's all a fucking illusion. The B-Specials are abolished and the UDR appear in their stead. And you see progress 'cause that's a world that makes sense to you. You're like the dehydrated man who sees the oasis in the desert, ending up with a mouthful of fucking sand. Catch yourself on, Ciarán. The Orange State is a creature with many limbs. The RUC, the DUP, the UUP, the UDA, the UFF, the UVF, the LVF, the Apprentice Boys, the B-Specials, the troops, the peelers, Stormont, Westminster, the whole fucking machine. We're just a bunch of fucking taigs to them, and nothing's ever going to change no matter how many different new acronyms you invent.

*There is a moment's silence.*

**Ciarán** Who did you kill Seán?

*SEÁN regards him carefully before speaking.*

**Seán** Do you know how to catch a peeler? You work out his routine. You establish where they go and at what time. That way the trap can be set, and nothing can go wrong. The clever ones would take different routes to work each day, check under their cars, avoid being seen in the same places on a regular basis. That's how it was. Routine is a killer.

**Ciarán** Seán, I don't like the way you're talking. You're not a Provo.

**Seán** Do you remember when I was seeing that midwife? Deirdre. She was training up at Altnagelvin Hospital.

**Ciarán** No. When was this?

**Seán** I must've been about eighteen. You probably don't remember.

**Ciarán** No. I don't.

**Seán** Well, I was seeing this midwife. Deirdre. As I say.

*SEÁN pauses. He seems uncomfortable.*

And I'd go up to Altnagelvin after her evening shift most nights, and I'd wait outside for her. 'Cause her shifts were erratic, so I could never be sure when she'd get off. Anyway, there was this man. Sitting outside on the same bench every night, chain-smoking. We'd got chatting a few times. Just small talk, you know. He'd give me the odd fag here and there, and we'd wait there together. Not that we had much in common, but it passed the time. His wife had some kind of kidney problem apparently. Anyway, he'd be there every night at that same time, sucking up that smoke on the same aul' bench. And one night, we got to talking. It was getting dark early, and I think he'd had a drink or two. It's funny how people open up when it gets dark. There's an atmosphere, isn't there? Like, like there's only now. And there's no consequences.

*There is a long pause.*

That's when he told me what he did for a living. I don't know why he told me. He knew I was from the Bogside. It was like, I don't know, I suppose he thought he could trust me.

**Ciarán** Jesus, Seán. He did trust you.

**Seán** No, not really. He just let his guard down. It was the drink, the dark. It wasn't me. (*Pause.*) But this fella. Well, he had a routine, didn't he? Because of his wife with the bad kidneys. (*Pause.*) So Malachy set it up. And when it was done do you know what he said to me? He said I was the stuff of a true volunteer.

**Ciarán** So you didn't in fact kill anyone at all, you merely set up the circumstances of their death.

**Seán**  It amounts to the same.

**Ciarán**  Aye, it does. But did you really think they'd let you join if you did this?

**Seán**  Why shouldn't they?

**Ciarán**  It seems to me they sussed you out a long time ago. They know your temperament. They know you'd be joining for the wrong reasons.

**Seán**  What the fuck is that supposed to mean?

**Ciarán**  It's not the country that's at stake here, Seán. It's your ego. You say you killed a man. An exaggeration to begin with, but it got my attention. This is just another wee tale for you to tell. You're boasting. You're proud.

**Seán**  And why shouldn't I be proud? I've made a lasting contribution to the movement.

**Ciarán**  What? By killing an innocent man?

**Seán**  Innocent? He was in the RUC! Probably in the UVF as well.

**Ciarán**  Probably in the UVF? You said he was.

**Seán**  Most of them were, you know.

**Ciarán**  No Seán, some of them were. You said you knew for sure. Can you even hear yourself? You're exaggerating everything until it's close enough to the story you want to tell. First you killed a member of the UVF. Now it seems you didn't kill anyone at all, and the man you set up wasn't a loyalist paramilitary in the first place. How many more changes can your wee story stand?

**Seán**  He worked for the security forces. He was a legitimate target.

**Ciarán** What does that even mean? (*With disdain.*) 'Legitimate target.' Who's got the right to make them choices? Not you, Seán, not anybody. Don't pretend this is about you fighting for your country. This is about you trying to suck up to the Provos because you want to feel part of it. (*Pause.*) This isn't us. This isn't what we stand for.

**Seán** Fuck up, Ciarán.

**Ciarán** (*After a moment's silence.*) What was his name?

**Seán** Who?

**Ciarán** Your man from the RUC.

**Seán** I'd rather not say.

**Ciarán** Why not?

**Seán** He was a uniform, not a name.

**Ciarán** The man in that uniform had a name. And a life. And a family. And memories. And feelings. (*Pause.*) You didn't kill the uniform, you just emptied it.

*SEÁN glowers at CIARÁN. There is a venomous silence.*

**Seán** Some things are worth it.

**Ciarán** Like what?

**Seán** Like liberating your land from a foreign government. Like breaking down artificial borders that cut our country in two.

**Ciarán** Is that what you think we've been doing?

**Seán** (*With an edge of bitterness.*) That's what we used to do.

**Ciarán** Well, maybe it all went too far. And maybe it's taken us thirty years to realise it.

**Seán** You don't understand.

**Ciarán**  Then explain to me, what exactly is it you're aspiring to? Is it revolution, or just the idea of revolution? You've seen those Palestinian flags flying at Free Derry Corner. And all that graffiti on the city walls supporting the Basque separatists, and leftist guerrillas in Colombia, and fuck knows what else. We're finding unity where it doesn't exist. These are different conflicts, different movements, and the only thing we've got in common is our ability to take life. Do you really think they're flying the tricolour in Gaza?

**Seán**  I hope there's a point to all this.

**Ciarán**  You're celebrating death, treating it like an ally. You enjoyed your wee story about that poor peeler, but that's all it was. A story. You had a man killed, but you didn't see a drop of blood.

*He points at THE CLOCK.*

That there. That's reality, so it is. Men like this don't tell stories, they live them. And men like you idolise them for it and beg to be involved. I don't want to play these games anymore. I want my stories to have happy endings.

*There is a pause. CIARÁN looks at his feet.*

(*Not looking up.*) I wish you hadn't told me about that RUC man.

**Seán**  Now that I've actually said it, it doesn't feel like a story anymore. It feels real.

**Ciarán**  Aye.

*An uncomfortable silence. SEÁN suddenly walks over to THE CLOCK in a decisive motion.*

**Seán**  I'm taking the mask off.

*He tries to do so. CIARÁN grabs his hands.*

**Ciarán**  Don't Seán. This isn't going to make anything better.

**Seán**  I have to know.

**Ciarán**  (*Insistent.*) Please. I can't see him. If I see that face, that face from my dreams…

**Seán**  So what if he is this Death-figure you've dreamt about? He's not Medusa. I won't turn to stone.

**Ciarán**  Eurynomus looked into the face of Death.

**Seán**  Who?

**Ciarán**  Eurynomus.

**Seán**  Another demon?

**Ciarán**  Not at first. He was a man. Flesh and blood. He met the Prince of Death in the underworld. But when he looked into his face, his soul vanished.

**Seán**  Is that supposed to scare me?

**Ciarán**  Please don't do this. You don't know what'll happen.

**Seán**  I'll pull this mask off, and we'll see one of Malachy's fellas, and that'll be the end of it. We untie him and do a runner. By the time he comes to, we'll be well away.

**Ciarán**  No, Seán.

**Seán**  If you don't want to see, then don't look.

**Ciarán**  Please don't do this. You'll regret it, I…

*SEÁN lifts the balaclava. CIARÁN turns and holds his hands over his eyes.*

Seán, stop it!

*SEÁN stares into THE CLOCK's face. He seems numbed. There is a moment's silence.*

Is it one of Malachy's men?

*No reply from SEÁN.*

Seán, is it one of them'ens?

**Seán**  (*Still numbed.*) No.

*He rolls the balaclava back over THE CLOCK's face.*

No. I've never seen him before in my life. (*Pause.*) You can look now, Ciarán. I've put the mask back on.

*CIARÁN slowly lowers his hands.*

**Ciarán**  So do you feel better?

**Seán**  Not at all.

*SEÁN picks up the alarm clock and stares at it.*

(*Quietly.*) What are you?

*He puts the alarm clock down and addresses THE CLOCK.*

You don't make sense here. See if you were anywhere else in the world you'd maybe fit in.

**Ciarán**  Seán…

**Seán**  (*Ignoring CIARÁN.*) But I know what you're trying to do. You being here trivialises everything. You're here to make us feel like there's something else, something beyond us. You want to make our own conflict feel insignificant. Because you're not a Catholic, or a Prod, or a Brit. You're just Death. And your targets aren't calculated, and there's no points to be scored. (*Pause.*) I'll not let you do it. I'll not let you belittle us like this.

*He picks up the hammer and raises it high above his head. We see the creature's view projected onto the screen, approaching the shack. It reaches the door. SEÁN struggles with himself, but cannot strike a blow. The projection fades. SEÁN begins to laugh. Lowering the hammer, he looks at CIARÁN, his expression almost pleading.*

Why can't I do it, Ciarán?

**Ciarán**  You know why.

**Seán**  Aye.

*He drops the hammer. There is a scratching noise at the door. A long pause. CIARÁN walks over to the door and opens it. The creature's view is projected as he does so. We see CIARÁN open the door and look directly at the creature. There is a moment of recognition. After a beat, CIARÁN slowly closes the door and the projection fades. He turns to SEÁN.*

What was that?

**Ciarán**  Nothing. Just a noise. It was nothing.

*CIARÁN picks up the bag of money.*

I think we should go now.

**Seán**  Go? Go where?

**Ciarán**  It doesn't matter. We should leave. We should just take what we have and just pretend he never came into our lives. Look…

*He hands the bag to SEÁN.*

We've got our money back now. This isn't our problem.

*SEÁN thinks about it.*

**Seán**  We'll be just grand, won't we?

**Ciarán**  Aye, we will. We don't need to kill anyone. We didn't see this man.

**Seán**  (*Nodding.*) That's right.

*SEÁN walks over to THE CLOCK and begins to untie his hands.*

We can leave together, so we can. We can make a fresh start. And we won't remember any of this. It'll be just like it was. And we won't have to run anymore. We can make our own choices.

**Ciarán**  Aye. This isn't our responsibility. We're not killers.

**Seán**  That's right.

*CIARÁN makes a decisive movement towards the exit. He stops at the door.*

**Ciarán**  Did he have a scar?

**Seán**  What?

**Ciarán**  When you looked at his face, I mean. (*Speaking slowly and mechanically.*) Did you see a long scar, irregular and deep, running from his right eye to the corner of his mouth?

**Seán**  (*Pause.*) No.

*CIARÁN smiles.*

**Ciarán**  Good.

*CIARÁN exits. SEÁN's expression is momentarily blank. He looks back at THE CLOCK, sustaining a vacant stare for a short while.*

(*Off.*) Are you coming, Seán?

**Seán**  (*Still numbed.*) Aye.

*After a pause, SEÁN exits. There is a gradual blackout. The creature's view is projected onto the screen. We see the shack from outside, as CIARÁN and SEÁN are leaving. The creature creeps into the shack and approaches THE CLOCK. There is a pause. THE CLOCK stirs. The projection fades.*

*The End.*